The Mexican American

The Mexican American

Advisory Editor
Carlos E. Cortés

LAW AND ORDER, LTD.

By
KYLE S. CRICHTON

ARNO PRESS
A New York Times Company
New York — 1974

Reprint Edition 1974 by Arno Press Inc.

Reprinted from a copy in The State Historical
Society of Wisconsin

THE MEXICAN AMERICAN
ISBN for complete set: 0-405-05670-2
See last pages of this volume for titles.

Manufactured in the United States of America

Library of Congress Cataloging in Publication Data

Crichton, Kyle Samuel, 1896-1960.
    Law and order, ltd.

    (The Mexican American)
    Reprint of the ed. published by New Mexican
Publishing Corp., Santa Fe.
    1. Baca, Elfego, 1864-1945. 2. Crime and
criminals—New Mexico. I. Title. II. Series.
F801.B15C7 1974   363.2'092'4 [B]   73-14200
ISBN 0-405-05674-5

LAW AND ORDER, LTD.

THE ROUSING LIFE OF ELFEGO BACA OF NEW MEXICO

By
KYLE S. CRICHTON, *1896-1960.*

SANTA FE
NEW MEXICAN PUBLISHING CORPORATION
1928

FOREWORD

In fashioning this life story of Elfego Baca we have made no attempt to set down in chronological order his deeds from birth to old age, but have been more concerned with those incidents which best bring out the interest and humor and strangeness of the Old West he lived in.

It is a method which has its faults, but it at least avoids those barren passages which often beclog the history of a man who is less than an international figure and yet is of sufficient importance to warrant writing about. The old method is apt to harrass the reader of any biographical work, and we can surely be pardoned for our lapse in continuity by our effort to present only the high lights of Mr. Baca's career.

We have been warned by friends who have read the book in manuscript that there will be difficulty by the layman—and particularly by the Easterner—in understanding the actions and psychology of such a man as Mr. Baca. They have pointed out the possibility of skepticism over such an episode as the one in which Mr. Baca blackens up with burnt cork and pursues the murderer Garcia, or of the other in which he gives away the stock of his cousin's store at Kelly. The only possible answer to this is that one who knows the romantic character of the Old Southwest and better still the romantic and *insouciant* attitude of those who stem from the Spanish will not only

find such things believable but quite logical. It
is the contrast of a figure such as Mr. Baca
against the conventional background of America
as it is now constituted which strikes us as unique
and worth writing about. Many a man has more
notches on his gun than Mr. Baca, but few have
carried themselves in their endeavors with the
same lightness of touch, the same off-hand qual-
ity of high courage.

From the closer friends of Mr. Baca, on the
other hand, is apt to come the complaint that many
incidents of his life have been overlooked. To this
charge we can only plead guilty and point again to
what we had to say in the first paragraph of this
introduction. In such incidents as the killing of
Policeman Maguire in Albuquerque by Kid Johnson and Charley Ross the part played by Elfego
Baca has not struck us as being of sufficient importance to merit inclusion. We were intrigued
for a time with the idea of proving Charley Ross
to be the Charley Ross of disappearance fame but
were forced regretfully to give it up through lack
of information. To Mr. Baca he was simply Charley Ross, a not particularly interesting gun
man of the second rank. If he were the real Charley Ross, said Mr. Baca in effect, he was assuredly
not worth discovery, and all the hullabaloo about
his disappearance was so much waste effort.

There is the further incident of the breaking
up of the Manzano gang—one of the outstanding

accomplishments of Mr. Baca's police record, but a matter more technical than entrancing and hence a trifle out of place in this book, as we have planned it. Half a dozen episodes of the same character could be elaborated upon, were there need of it.

There has been no intention, to go further, of making this a complete picture of the Old Southwest. It is a section which still possesses a fascination quite unknown elsewhere in America and it retains numerous citizens who helped make its thrilling history under early American rule. New Mexico is at once the oldest and newest portion of the United States and there is something about the grandeur of its mountains and the barrenness of its *mesas* which compels romance. Its background of Indian and Spanish *Conquistadore* culture is joined with the early American and Mexican influence in a way which creates atmosphere and allurement. We have been conscious of Elfego Baca's position in this setting and have realized the part he has played in the history of his native state, but we have not felt it within our province to elaborate upon the scene in which he moved.

We have tried to check up faithfully on all items which enter into this history and feel that we have succeeded in all but those instances in which we have made it clear in the course of the narrative that we are doubtful. We have felt it our duty to include several of the legends which have grown up about the figure of Billy the Kid without attempting to claim authenticity for them. They are included because they are good stories and because they have a bearing on some action in this life of our present hero.

We were on the point of saying that our only hope for this book is that you would find it read able. That, however, is a sample of false modesty which we shall not be able to cling to. In truth we are hopeful that this history of Elfego Baca will find its way into those important collections of *Americana* which concern themselves with the Southwest.

We expect some remonstrance over the facts in this volume. As we say later in its pages, there is always some difference of opinion to be expected between the shooter and the relatives of the shootee. In extenuation of the facts as set down we can only say that we have striven mightily to keep them straight.

If you complain that we have favored the shooter in our accounts, we can only remind you that we have after all been writing the history of the shooter and not the shootee—and that the shooter is still alive and active.

KYLE S. CRICHTON,
Albuquerque, N. M., Sept., 1927.

CHAPTER ONE
ELFEGO IS CAPTURED BY THE INDIANS

*"If there is one to be buried and one to be tried;
I'm going to be the one to be tried."*
—Philosophy of Elfego Baca.

A good western story always begins with the
Indians. So it is legitimate enough to say that
Elfego Baca was captured by the Indians at
Estancia at the age of one. Which leads naturally
enough to the question: "Who is Elfego Baca?"
And the story is launched almost before you know
it.

The name of Elfego Baca has been potent for
more than forty years in all of New Mexico and
that part of Texas which centers about El Paso.
That it is known only fleetingly elsewhere is no
fault of Elfego Baca's. The trouble with writing
his life is that you're bound to be a victim no matter what you say. Tolerance and fleeting years
have made a difference, but there was a day ten
years gone when the mention of the name of Mr.
Baca was excuse enough for anybody to draw
forth a gavel and demand that the meeting come
to order. It was a sign for debate. It was a case
of being either for or against Elfego Baca and if
you were against him it was just as well to keep
the news from the gentleman himself.

When Secretary Fall entered the Department

of Interior in 1920, he found several situations which required a strong hand. There was for one the matter of the Piute Indians in Southern Utah who for years had ruled their little section and dared any white man to come near. In addition they had formed the habit of dropping down from their domain and returning with the live stock of their reluctant American neighbors below. The matter of compensation was not mentioned.

"I've got the man for this," said Fall, and forthwith despatched a message to New Mexico.

In due course a gentleman of fair rotundity and a mild, humorous countenance put in his appearance at the office of the Secretary of Interior. The assistant secretaries who knew the Piutes and did not know Elfego Baca took several long looks at Mr. Baca and then went to consult with Secretary Fall.

"Mr. Fall," they said. "We know this Mr. Baca is a personal friend of yours and in the circumstances we feel it our duty to inform you that he is taking a terrible . . . . . ."

"A terrible risk!" said Fall cutting in. "Elfego taking a terrible risk! You make me laugh."

"But, Mr. Fall," they protested. "Mr. Baca looks like a very amiable and estimable gentleman, true enough, but you don't know these Piutes."

"The Piutes don't know Elfego, either," said

Secretary Fall. "You save your sympathies for the Piutes."

And Elfego Baca started for Southern Utah with the badge of authority pinned to his left suspender and with no orders except to get to the Piutes and bring them to time. It is not an especially thrilling story when compared with earlier ones of Elfego's life, and we'll not go into it. The Salt Lake newspapers made a great to-do about the feat of Mr. Baca and published his picture with fulsome words of praise.

The incident is important in bringing Elfego Baca down to date. The gentleman was alive in 1920 and he is still very much alive today. He is, as ever, amiable and jolly and rotund and his age is no longer what it was back in 1890, for example, but there is yet no general anxiety among residents of New Mexico to rush up and cast fiery words into the teeth of Mr. Baca—if you gather our meaning.

But to begin with the Indians in 1865 when Elfego was at the tender age of one year. Historians of greater or less repute for veracity have given it that the Navajo practice of the period in regard to puling white infants was to treat them to a fairly efficient boiling in oil or to grasp them nimbly by the heels and dash their brains out against a nearby rock. It sounds shocking enough —true or otherwise—but hold your seats, dear paying patrons. Nothing disastrous happened in the case of our hero, Elfego.

Master Baca was returned to his parents at the end of two days none the worse for his experience. This constitutes, according to Mr. Baca and his friends, the first incident in a long and agitated career which entitled him to the subsequent tag of "charmed." Detractors of Mr. Baca contend just as forcibly—but outside the presence and earshot of Mr. Baca—that the infant Elfego was boiled in oil for two days with nothing resulting but a lovely pink hue denoting the best of health and that he rebounded at such a pace when swung against the rock as to quite upset—literally and figuratively—the good chieftain who had undertaken the pleasurable deed.

As you go on, you will note this persistent conflict between what *is* the truth and what is thought to be. This is probably not the proper manner to begin a serious biography, but it is perhaps as good a way as any to indicate the difference of opinion and great variation of interpretation of events likely in this great work—the life story of the last of the straight shooters of the West—a character whose name has meant everything in his native State of New Mexico during the past 40 years. There is, naturally, a difference of opinion to be expected between the shooter, let us say, and the shootee—or his near relatives.

In Socorro County, New Mexico, forty years

ago when Elfego roamed it first as an adventur-
ous youth and later as sheriff, there was apt to be
a surplusage of high and lofty revolver work, and
it was just as sensible to get your day's endeavor
over effectively as to waste time on explanation,
apology or false regrets. The best explanation,
naturally, was a rapid draw, and there would be
plenty of time later to have friendly words with
the judge in case the affair ever reached that
stage.

Socorro County, up to five years ago, was
rather a roomy nation in its own right. In area
it was approximately three times the size of Al-
sace-Lorraine, twice the size of Wales, and with
approximately equal combustibility with one of
the more heated Balkan States. Life was very
carefree and gay and sudden. Tuesday you were
here—Wednesday where were you? Like that.

But Elfego was to know little of Socorro until long after the Indians finished with him at
Estancia. Estancia was only a stopping place on
the trail back to Kansas. The Baca family was
part of an ox team headed East. Father Baca,
bitten either with a desire to get his family to civilization while breath remained intact within them
or, as his son Elfego reports, eager to give his
family the benefits of education that Socorro did
not offer, Father Baca, we say, was headed for
Topeka, Kansas, and a desultory existence as a
minor contractor. Fourteen years of it, they stood,

and it is no part of this history to go into this weary period of Elfego Baca's life. It ended with the death of the mother.

Father Baca stayed behind in Topeka to close up his affairs. Elfego and his brother, Abdenago, proceeded on to Socorro to live with an uncle until their father arrived. Elfego was fifteen and an alien in his home town. His Spanish was that picked up from a Spanish household and diffused through the rough hewn English of a Kansas community. It was very poor Spanish, and Elfego was in the position of a man who returns from the wars to find his sweetheart afraid of him. Not that Elfego suffered the pangs of inferiority as a result of his lingual difficulties. There might be smiles and ridicule but they were of a furtive nature—not exposed to the bright gaze of Elfego. Kansas may not have aided the mental or moral development of young Baca, but it had helped him physically. He was not fair meat for boys his own age.

His career began rather auspiciously a year later upon the return of his father and the subsequent assuming by that gentleman of the role of Town Marshal of Belen. Father Baca was also of sporting enough inclinations to possess a quarter horse that very rudely shattered the hopes of a prominent citizen of Los Lunas, of a powerful family in the state of New Mexico. The shattering was followed by words and combat that led to the

Elfego Baca shortly after his return to Socorro from Topeka, Kansas, and just before his rescue of his father from the Los Lunas jail.

gentleman returning to Los Lunas with his face bashed into a strange and curious contour. Father Baca, fresh from the freedom of Kansas, was not of a type to admire the gentleman from Los Lunas. His words to that effect and his rude usage of the gentleman were considered very gravely in the councils of the great family and placed carefully in the black books of their clan.

In the discharge of his duties as town marshal some time later, Father Baca went so far in his zeal for law and order as to dispatch to eternity two cow punchers who were seeking to make Belen their happy play ground. Father Baca, to his surprise, was haled off to jail, tried by the court at Los Lunas, and sentenced to a stay of considerable duration in the State Penitentiary.

This was not considered "cricket" in the Baca family, which was firmly of the mind that their parent was not being treated exactly as befitted a hero and a town marshal. Especially disturbed was young Elfego. In addition to being disturbed, he was angry, hurt, ashamed and resentful. This was, said Elfego in so many words, no way to treat the father of Elfego Baca. He started to Los Lunas from Socorro to see what could be done about it. Strangely, he selected a day for his arrival in Los Lunas when the jailer would be engaged with matters having to do with his offices as a good Catholic. It was, to be exact, the feast day of Saint Teresa, and there was time to be spent in church, time to be spent after church in celebration. It would be a question of prayers before a candle illuminated effigy and frequent sips of wine for the better part of the night.

With Efego was young Chavez. They reached Belen from Socorro with a total of forty-five cents. Walking, to a western reared boy, has always been a mild form of disgrace, but, for the honor of family Baca and the confutation of those who arrested Father Baca, the necessary nine miles between Belen and Los Lunas were traversed on foot.

They found the jail on the first floor of a rambling two-storied adobe which housed the court room as a second floor. The cell of Father Baca lay directly beneath the second floor room to which the jury retired for deliberations. Elfego went around to the *placitas* at the rear of the structure and secured a ladder used for window washing. Placing it against the side of the court house and jail, he ascended to the jury room, crept through the easily opened window, and proceeded, with the aid of Chavez, to saw out a space in the floor large enough for the body of Father Baca to wiggle through from beneath. It was leisurely work. The jailer was gone for the night; it was midnight and they were too far from the habitations of Los Lunas to occasion suspicion by the sawing. They sawed until the last board creaked through and they could see Father Baca waiting patiently below.

Two fellow prisoners boosted Father Baca through the opening and were in turn boosted and yanked through to freedom. With this done, there was ample time to think of making a getaway. Young Elfego returned the ladder politely to its place in the *placitas* and spent such time as was necessary in stripping the clothes line of the jailer of the jerked venison hanging thereon. With it came ears of corn and chili—food enough for a fair-sized cavalcade. Amply stocked, the five—Father Baca, the two other prisoners, Elfego and young Chavez—walked calmly across the road to a clump of high grass approximately seventy-five feet from the jail and courthouse entrance. The first faint rays of the sun were struggling over the horizon. It was four o'clock in the morning.

In the high grass within easy access of the hubbub at the county jail, the five munched jerked meat, corn, chili and watermelons from the field they were lying in, and watched with considerable interest through the long day while the sheriff and deputy sheriffs and posses of great size and indignation started out from the jail entrance and beat the surrounding country with energy and abandon in search of the gentlemen who had so grossly dishonored the stability of the Valencia County *carcel*. There were hullabaloos and shouts and strenuous flauntings of deadly weapons.

"The culprits," declared the stern voice of the sheriff which carried beautifully to the pop-eyed spectators in the high grass, "the culprits must be apprehended for the honor of good old Valencia County." Or words to that effect. The culprits wettened their faces with another bite of luscious Valencia County watermelon and nodded grave assent to the sheriff's determination. Determination was part of a good sheriff's stock in trade. The culprits would have been chagrined to be outwitting a sheriff who had neither determination nor effectiveness. It was reasonably certain that he was to fall short in effectiveness. It was entirely necessary that he should retain determination.

It was rather a nice day for young Elfego. He had more to eat than was good for him, but he had the pleasure of checking out the posses as they left the jail and checking them in again as they returned, weary and a bit dejected, from scouring the mountains and beating up and down the banks of the silvery Rio Grande. The experience gained then was to be of service to him later when, as sheriff, he picked up criminals within ear shot of the site of their crimes rather than credit them with airplane hops away from there. The average criminal, quoth Mr. Baca in his more mature years, is generally unable to get away rapidly from the scene of his devilment and, wisely, is often unwilling to do same.

After dark the Baca picnicing party broke up and prepared for departure. The two fellow prisoners headed North for Albuquerque, Father Baca, Elfego and Young Chavez started South for Escondida, three miles north of the town of Socorro. At Escondida, they dropped Young Chavez and secured three horses and a guide who knew the way to Old Mexico. There was no rush now. They were in the bosom of their own family. There were uncles to the right of them, nephews to the left. At the first approach of a strange face, the community would have arisen in behalf of the Baca connection. At the end of four days, they proceeded on to Socorro, Texas, which was in turn but half of Socorro, Old Mexico. Father Baca spent a period of seven years with a brother who kept a store at Ysleta, Texas, near El Paso. He returned at the end of that time to be a respected citizen of his native county.

It is a charming characteristic of the Southwest that time works slowly in making its changes. Though the Los Lunas episode was forty years ago, you can still see the self same court house and jail. But you will not see them as court house and jail, but as the Los Lunas Hotel, owned and operated by its genial proprietor of Greek parentage, George Ade. No less. Mr. Ade will be happy to lead you upstairs to the ex-jury room—now a guest chamber—and show you the cuts in the floor—still there—from the eager saw of young

Elfego Baca. He will reveal for your interest the low jury room window through which operations were begun and finished. And from the window of the now famous guest room he will point out to you across the road the high grass where the Baca picnic party spent the day of rest and entertainment.

If you perchance should revisit the old scene in the presence of the hero himself—as we did—you should be prepared to hear many tales in addition to the one that concerns him. You will, for example, be properly shocked on eating in the tiny restaurant of proprietor Ade to be told that here —right in this very room, that was then a part of the *placitas*—nine men were hanged in a single night from one staunch *viga*.

"You know a *viga*," says Mr. Baca, flattering us. A *viga* in short is what we know as a rafter or cross piece to hold up a building.

"The tree in the back yard," puts in Mr. Ade, with historical seal. "Four men were hung on it in one night."

We have become, in our time, a great deal more avid of life, you will reflect when thinking of olden days in New Mexico. Forty years is a long time. Gone are Billy the Kid, Joe Fowler, Henry Coleman, Wild Bill Hickok, Black Jack Ketcham, Kid Johnson. There remains Elfego Baca, friend of them all except Wild Bill Hickok who lived in a different territory, confidant of many, protector of a few and responsible for bringing others to justice. The bad days are done. A killing now is of far greater moment in New Mexico than in Chicago or New York. In this year of grace, 1927, a murder trial in New Mexico is a thing to wonder about. They are few, they are scarce, they are something to be regarded with awe. In the early days of Elfego, they were as common as Fourth of July inebriates. There were lawyers for the defense, and special lawyers to aid the prosecu tion. An attorney had as much chance to make a fee out of the prosecution as out of the defense. The friends of the slain gentleman insisted that his honor be vindicated. In the courtroom went on the technicalities of law with the precision of the most correct court in the land. In the jury box there was one test of guilt. ''Did the deceased have a fair chance?'' If the deceased had a fair chance in a fair fight, there was nothing to do but acquit the prisoner and shake him warmly by the hand as a gallant man. Did the prisoner shoot the deceased in the back without warning? Hang the prisoner as high as Haman, with the very best regards of the jury.

CHAPTER TWO

ELFEGO MEETS BILLY THE KID AND LEARNS OF JUSTICE

Elfego knew Billy the Kid as a boy. Billy the Kid, at the time of his death from the gun of Sheriff Pat Garrett of Lincoln County, had barely reached the age of twenty. At the time the two rode from Socorro to Albuquerque, Elfego was sixteen and Billy the Kid about seventeen. They put up their horses at Isleta, the pueblo Indian village thirteen miles from Albuquerque, and walked into town. There was cheap stabling at Isleta with the Indians and your horse was safe— which it was not in Albuquerque or elsewhere. Billy had not yet begun his famous career, but he was already known as Billy the Kid because of his boyish face and his tall, slim, almost feminine figure. Part of the fascination in the life of Billy the Kid lies in the fact that he was not a bruiser, but rather the Knight Errant, a David against the Goliaths of the law. He was lightning fast and debonair with it all. Billy the Kid had an air about him, a way about him, and there are still sedate men living in the west who profess anything but admiration for the way in which Pat Garrett is said to have surprised Billy the Kid and killed him in the dark.

But Billy Bonney—whose last name, by the way, is yet unknown to many men who knew him personally—was at the time he came to Albuquerque a young man with only the customary record of deviltry behind him. He was carefree, he was gay, and he was loose in the metropolis of the state.

His conception of justice—whatever it might have been hitherto—received an immediate lesson in Albuquerque. Elfego and Billy the Kid had straggled to a position of rest beside a telegraph pole on First street after a walk which was not pleasant to young men footed in highheeled cowboy boots and as avid of pedestrianism as a seal of roller skating. They rested beside the friendly telegraph post and surveyed the street—deserted save for a man talking to a policeman and a third man walking near them.

When the third man was ten steps past, the policeman hailed him.

"Hey!" he said sharply, and the man turned. The policeman shot at the same instant, and the walker curled to the boardwalk and was still. Simultaneously, the man accompanying the policeman dragged forth his revolver and shot directly into the air. In almost the same motion, he ran toward the man lying quietly on the sidewalk. Very cleverly he placed the smoking revolver in the dead man's hands and was kneeling in an attitude of solicitation when crowds burst from nearby saloons and dashed down side streets at the sound of shots.

"He tried to get me," said the policeman modestly. "I got the draw on him." The man who fired the shot aimlessly in the air nodded agreement. As he got up Elfego saw he had in his hand the untouched revolver which had been in the holster of the dead man. He placed it carelessly in his own holster as if further need for it was ended. The desperado was dead. Justice was vindicated. It would teach other men not to have a grudge against a policeman who was quick on the draw. Elfego and Billy the Kid wandered off slowly in the direction of Old Town meditating on the strange ways of justice.

Old Town was the Old Town of most western towns of the period. It was larger and accordingly wilder, and activity focussed in great part in the old Martinez Bar—famous from Denver to El Paso and points west. The old Martinez Bar was a long, low adobe building. A bar room ran along the length of one side and the remainder of the room was taken up with roulette tables, faro tables, black jack tables, and tables for draw and stud poker. It was a right lively sight—was the Martinez Bar in the days Billy the Kid roamed.

Billy knew exactly how he could endear himself to the male and peculiar female patrons of the Old Martinez for Billy the Kid had cultivated the mysterious art of pounding the ivories. In the forgotten days of his youth a fond mother had headed him in the direction of a piano and he had improved on his few lessons since. There are modest homesteads in New Mexico to this day that recall with abounding pleasure the lithesome, gentle, almost girlish young man in chaps and with guns hanging prominently, who stopped at the ranch for a drink or a bite to eat and paid for it with marvelous renditions of "Turkey in the Straw," 'Swanee River" and "Old Folks at Home."

It was marvelous playing that Billy the Kid did. There can be no mistake about that. Anything would have been marvelous to the musically starved ranchers and their even more intellectually starved women folk. How well he played is really a matter of doubt. Probably Billy the Kid played only passably. There will never be conviction on the point. It is enough to know that the slight, romantic young man played in a manner to wring the hearts of the women in desolate ranch houses. It is almost enough to excuse him for the few cattle he stole, for the few men he killed in the course of his rambles. He was the Fairy Prince of New Mexico in many hearts, and there were as many hearts who never knew the name and reputation of the young fellow who smiled amiably while he brought tunes from a piano or tiny parlor organ that had been dragged laboriously across mountains and plains by expensive ox-team freight and had perhaps scarcely been touched since its arrival.

We say, then, that in Martinez Bar Billy the Kid could have easily placed himself in an enviable position by merely walking to the poor battered piano and wrenching from it its few remaining chords. He was either not in the mood for music or the recent experience on First Street, new Albuquerque, had not endeared him to mankind. Instead, he and Elfego strolled about among the tables, being careful not to get too close to the hands being played and yet amply close enough to see how fortune was moving. They had drinks at the bar and they looked about carelessly. They discovered with little or no trouble the location of the chief bouncer. This gentleman, bearing a long, soupy, drooping mustache, was paid by the owners of Martinez Bar and supplied by the county with a deputy sheriff badge. He looked hardboiled; he looked efficient, he looked almost as if he might be a person a little, if anything, over anxious in his regard for law and order. During the course of their inspection Elfego and Billy the Kid saw him oust several inebriated gentlemen with more force than tact.

It was late afternoon and things were dull. They wandered out and into other saloons and gambling houses and ate a leisurely supper. They returned to the Martinez at the height of its glory along about ten o'clock. The bar was lined, the tables were filled, the dance hall in connection was getting a fair play. The droopy mustachioed bouncer was keen of eye, alert, on the hop. The honor of good old Martinez Bar seemed especially dear to him that evening.

Billy the Kid possessed a revolver of curious make. It was short and stubby and had the look, almost, of a toy gun that shoots water instead of lead. It had the air of a sawed-off shotgun, and made, when shot, the noise of a falling load of bricks. The room was jammed; the crowd was milling about; there was noise and loud drinking talk. In the midst of it Billy the Kid pulled out his abbreviated pistol and fired three times into the rafters of Old Martinez Bar.

"POW! POW! POW!"

Elfego knew that Billy the Kid fired the shots because he had been forewarned in that regard. Billy the Kid also knew it because he had fired the shots. But nobody else knew it, and even Elfego didn't know where the revolver went after the shots were fired. The reaction was very complete and satisfying to a young man just starting out in the world. Bartenders dropped precipitately behind their wooden protection. Strong men slid into corners and out through handy doors. Bedecked females of few morals and approximately as many garments uttered screams more frantic than feminine and clung to monied patrons. Tables were shoved back, cards were lost and games were definitely interrupted.

Be it eternally said to the credit of our friend the bouncer, he was on the job. He had not seen the shots fired, he had no idea who fired the shots, but one look into the flying mob gave him a fair idea. He was helped, it must be admitted, by the fact that of all in the room Billy the Kid was calmest, most unruffled, most urbane. In a man of his slight physique and boyish appearance, such action was not ordinary; such action, in few words, was suspicious—very damned suspicious, said the bouncer with the droopy menacing mustache.

"Who fired that gun!" demanded the bouncer bearing down upon Billy the Kid and Elfego, who, forewarned, had left his gun outside.

"What gun?" queried Billy the Kid, innocently, suavely, unworriedly.

"You know dam well what gun," declared the bouncer in accents harsh and earnest.

"Why, I haven't even *got* a gun," said Billy the Kid, with a hurt air of injured innocence.

The bouncer knew the one sure way to find out. He wasted no additional words, feeling himself on strange ground when it came to repartee, and firmly convinced that the only repartee worth its salt was a forty-five in vigorous action. He proceeded to search our evening's hero, Billy. He searched him high and he searched him low. He searched in holsters, in boots, in rear pockets, in the not particularly spotless shirt of Billy the Kid. He searched and accepted the support of an extraordinarily bold bartender, who also put in licks of searching,—but without success. There was no gun in or about the unconcerned young man who waited patiently while they pawed over him. They gave it up. They walked away with the suspicion of a grumble. They were not polite about it, and they offered no apologies for putting the young man to annoyance. The young man seemed not put out because of it.

"Have a drink," he said amiably to the glowing bouncer.

"You go to hell!" said that gentleman crossly, "and keep that gun out of sight if you don't want hopped out of here on your ear."

"What gun?" said Billy the Kid leaning gently against the bar and smiling with the patience one gives to a naughty but muchly beloved child.

The bouncer was in danger of chewing off his mustache with mortification. He disappeared from sight to regain his composure. Billy and Elfego continued to stroll about leisurely and things in the old Martinez Bar returned to normal.

They leaned against the wall near a game of draw poker. Suddenly Elfego felt the nudge of cold steel against his side. He jumped, and wheeled to face Billy.

"Where'd you have that gun?" he whispered tensely at sight of it.

"Sh-h! whispered Billy the Kid in return, strolling off toward the center of the room again. Suddenly the din was pierced, exactly as the first time, by three sudden shots into the rafters.

"POW! POW! POW!"

No one, seemingly, saw the gun come out; no one saw it disappear. It was simply a case of three rapid shots from nowhere fired by nobody. In reading this you must remember that Billy the Kid, as soon to be revealed to all the world that cared to notice, was one of the most miraculous sleight of hand men with a revolver ever to trod hard earth. He was to be known as "forked lightning" with a pistol. That he made use of it later with dire results to people who came between his gun and daylight was not to say that he could manipulate a revolver more rapidly afterwards than now in the confines of Old Martinez Bar. That the shots had been fired into the rafters by the slight young man who stood modestly in the middle of the room and calmly surveyed the havoc, mental and physical, he had wrought,—that he had done this, we say, there was no longer doubt in many minds. He of the droopy mustachio came on the dead lope to make way with this smart aleck who thought he could shoot up the old Martinez Bar without remorse to himself.

"Come on!" bellowed droopy.

"Why?" said Billy calmly, with the same injured air.

"Why!" howled droopy. "Shootin' yer damned gun in here! *Why?* You git, now, and no dam monkey shines!"

"I haven't even *got* a gun," said Billy, sadly, mournfully.

"You ain't goin' ta fool me no more," yelled old droopy. "Git! I tell you!"

"Now, wait," said a soothing, softly menacing voice. "The boy says he ain't got no gun. You ain't goin' to throw him out for nothing!"

The interceder was not asking a question; he was saying politely that old droopy wasn't going to throw out Billy the Kid unless he had something on him. The intruder would, very efficiently, see to that.

They went through the business of searching Billy the Kid a second time. He submitted to it patiently even when Old Droopy was assisted by half the staff of Old Martinez Bar. There was equal success to the first attempt. In short; none. By this time Billy the Kid had gathered about him supporters of some calibre. There was no likelihood that Old Droopy would do anything rash with a view of depositing Billy in the alley way. Billy the Kid and Elfego strolled about for half an hour later before hitting for the great Open Spaces.

Once in the free ozone, Elfego burst forth with the agitation that had threatened to overwhelm him within the confines of Old Martinez Bar.

"Where's that gun! he asked.

"Here!" said the nonchalant Billy, taking off his sombrero with a flourish and tossing the weapon forth. And so it was. The stumpy Colt had rested on the famous pate of Billy the Kid under the protecting shelter of the ample head-gear furnished by Mr. John B. Stetson of Phila-delphia. It had been a case of three rapid "POWS!" into the roof of the old Martinez Bar and a lightning, quicker-than-the-eye toss of the pistol under the hat. It was very simple for Billy the Kid. For others less agile, it would have re-sulted in a severe bouncing into the street near old Martinez Bar and at least slight lacerations where he alighted.

CHAPTER THREE

ELFEGO WINS HIS REPUTATION AT FRISCO

The Albuquerque experience was of great value, great inspiration to young Elfego Baca, of Socorro. He returned home something of a man of the world. He had taken part in the confounding of tyranny; he had witnessed the perversion of justice; and he had grown to the stature of man almost over night. From Billy the Kid he had learned manipulations of a revolver that were vouchsafed few mortals. He was what might be called a hefty young man, with a piercing, steady eye, a bolted rapidity of draw, and a disdainful lack of fear that has remained with him steadily to this day. As this is written, you will meet many people in New Mexico who have anything but a favorable opinion of Elfego Baca, but you will meet none who deny him the attributes of courage.

He was about to enter upon the adventure that definitely established his reputation in the Southwest.

The town of Frisco in Western Socorro County was a tiny Mexican settlement with an Upper Plaza, Middle Plaza and Lower Plaza. Now known as Reserve and County seat of Catron County and 90 miles from a railroad, it was then the happy romping ground of certain outfits of Texas cowpunchers who spent their Saturday evenings and holidays in taking pot shots at the populace who had been so unfortunate as to come within range of their limber six shooters. It was especially at the mercy of the hired employes of one Slaughter, who yearly drove his herds through from Texas to Western Socorro, picking up what stray native cattle happened to be in the way and finally arriving at his ranch near Frisco with considerable new wealth.

There had been remonstrance about this, but no action, for the Slaughter outfit was well heeled and a bit rough and quick on the trigger. There was even less remonstrance among the terror-stricken inhabitants of Frisco. Should the Justice of Peace seek so far to retain his legal dignity as to incarcerate one of the offenders, it would be simply an excuse for the jolly Slaughter boys to come down and practice target shooting at his fleeing form and to kick open the jail and take out their little pal. The Slaughter outfit, in short, was a law unto itself.

It was into this atmosphere that young Elfego Baca strayed one day in the fall of 1884, with no intent in mind other than to look things over and visit friends.

It is as well to quote now directly from Mr. J. H. Cook's book "Fifty Years on the Old Frontier", published in 1923 by the Yale University Press. Mr. Cook took part in the occurrence, the facts of which have been substantiated numerous times, especially in the testimony of the several murder trials arising out of the fracas.

Mr. Cook says: "It appeared that on the previous day a cowboy named McCarty, employed by Mr. Slaughter, a cattleman holding some stock a few miles from the Plaza, had ridden into the Upper Plaza. Securing a few drinks of liquor at a store kept by a man named Milligan, he had proceeded to shoot up the place. Riding back and forth in the street, he shot at everything, animate and inanimate, which met his gaze. While the drunken cowboy was thus engaged, a young Mexican named Elfego Baca rode into the Plaza. He was a special deputy sheriff from the County Seat of Socorro County, and he was out on an electioneering trip, making speeches in the various Mexican settlements of the county.

"McCarty, the drunken cowboy, did not notice Baca's arrival, but Baca had noticed him. Meeting the Justice of Peace and some of the other residents of the Plaza, Baca asked them why they allowed the cowboy to jeopardize their lives and property in such manner. The reply was that, if they arrested or harmed McCarty, his friends would come and do a lot of harm to the settlement. Baca told them that when such things were tolerated it only made the cowboys bolder, and that it should be stopped at once. He insisted that they should not let the Americans living among them get the impression that the Mexicans were afraid of them. He further informed them that he was a peace officer, that it was his duty to stop McCarty from endangering the lives of the citizens of the place, and that he would show McCarty there was at least one Mexican in the country who was not afraid of an American cowboy.''

We must interrupt Mr. Cook at this point to clear up a few things as we go along. Young Baca, with the ever present urge for law enforcement, was a deputy sheriff self appointed. He was aged nineteen at the time, and his badge was one of the sort now ladled out by detective correspondence schools. It was not the badge of a deputy sheriff of Socorro or any other County, but it was enough of a badge to convince Frisco amid the excitement. It was the fact of his assumption of office that he did not possess that brought him within the toils of the law when the affair was concluded. But to go on with Mr. Cook's excellent narrative:

''Baca went out at once and arrested and disarmed McCarty with but little trouble; for he was really not a bad man—merely a little too playful at times. Taking his prisoner before the Justice of Peace in the Plaza, Baca was informed by his Honor that he did not care to hear the case, as there would surely be an aftermath which would result badly for the Plaza. Baca replied that, in such a case, where the Justice seemed intimidated, he considered it his own duty to take his prisoner to the County Seat, where the case could be tried.

"As it was too late for Baca to start at once for the town of Socorro, he decided to remain with the prisoner in the Mexican settlement overnight. He took McCarty down to the Middle Plaza, where there was more suitable accommodations for himself and his prisoner. By some means word of McCarty's arrest had gone out from the Plaza. A number of Mr. Slaughter's cowboys, headed by Mr. Perham, their foreman, rode down at once to the place where Baca was holding McCarty and demanded his release. When Baca was informed that the prisoner would be taken from him right then and there, he told them that he would give them the time it would take to count three to get out of town. Baca counted 'one, two, three' and opened fire on the Americans with his pistol. The Slaughter cowboys started to get out of harm's way very suddenly. By some chance, Mr. Perham's horse fell and killed its rider. One of the Americans, Allen by name, was shot by Baca through the knee. Baca held to his prisoner."

By this time, if we may be allowed to stop Mr. Cook again, things in Upper, Middle and Lower Frisco were churned to a pretty state. The shock received by the Slaughter representatives in coming to relieve young Elfego of the responsibility of his prisoner and getting his curt order to depart before he had completed his arithmetic to

the extent of "three", was almost more of a stun-
ner than the fact of Perham's unfortunate crush-
ing by his falling horse. It was enough to start
couriers in all directions to round up the "Ameri-
canos" to the defense of their heaven-sent rights.
It was such a courier who dashed up to the ranch
house of Mr. Cook at a furious gait and called hurriedly that the Mexicans had gone on the warpath
at Frisco and that they were trying to wipe out all
the Americans living near the settlement. He
rushed on to carry the news to others, much like
Paul Revere of old, though in not so worthy a
cause. Cook arrived at the Plaza to find the Mexicans as docile and cowed as ever and the source
of all the "uprising" and the massacre of all the
Americans to lie in the person of young Baca, who
clung steadfastly to his prisoner and his determination. The Mexicans at all times kept well out
range of trouble, being greatly outnumbered by
the cowboys and helpless before them. They left
Elfego to fight his own battles. But to get back
to Cook again:

"We held a council and decided to select one
or two of our number to go to the Plaza, see the
Justice of the Peace and Mr. Baca, and try to
arrange for the trial of McCarty at the Plaza; for
the charge against him was not a desperately serious one, and we all realized that considerable
trouble might be started. Our committee waited
upon the Justice and Mr. Baca, and they agreed to

The famous *jacal* at Frisco where Elfego held eighty Texas cowboys at bay for 33 hours, killing four, wounding eight, and coming through unscathed himself.

our suggestion. Mr. Baca stated that he would have the prisoner at the Justice's office at the stated hour. The crowd which I was with, and which, the evidence later showed, was composed of eighty men, then rode down to the Upper Plaza at the time appointed for the trial. Baca had McCarty at the Justice's office. After taking his prisoner inside, he came out and greeted us, saying 'Good morning, Gentlemen'.''

We must depart with Mr. Cook here definitely, for things were about to happen at a pace not to be taken at the leisurely gait of reminiscence forty years later. The Slaughter outfit, with the death of Perham fresh in its mind, was in no mood for either fair play or polite words. Despite the efforts of Cook, Clement Hightower, and Jerome Martin—all known to Baca—who had arranged for the truce and bringing of McCarty for trial, the Slaughter cavalcade was not to be soothed. As Baca brought up McCarty to the Justice of the Peace's office, he was met by the horde of Slaughter—80 in number, as later testified to at the trial—who swung up from the arroyo by the office, and swept down upon young Baca standing by the corner of the building. It was then that he addressed the crowd, as related by Cook.

"Good morning, Mr. Wilson," said Baca affably.

"Good morning, you dirty Mexican blankety blank," replied Wilson in turn, following it up by words of like purport. It was then also that a shot was fired by one of the Slaughter crowd.

It was then, also, that Baca drew out his guns, covered the closest of the Slaughter outfit and backed hastily through an alleyway to the protection of a tiny *jacal* that stood in a clearing at the end of the lane. He found there a woman and her two boys.

"Vamos!" yelled Baca. "Get out before you're killed!"

Close on Elfego's heels had come the Slaughter outfit, headed by Jim Herne, a Texan with a bounty over his head and disdain for Mexicans in his heart. He got off his horse, dragged his rifle from its position on the saddle and advanced toward the *jacal* inhabited by Baca.

"I'll get this dirty little Mexican out of here," he said. "Come on, you", he bellowed. "Come out of there, and come damned quick!"

Baca's answer was two revolver shots, both of which hit vital spots. Either of them was enough to kill Herne, and one did. Friends bore the body away hastily and the siege was on.

It was none o'clock in the morning, and young Elfego Baca was at bay, with eighty of the roughest, sharpest shooting Texas cowboys in history facing him from easy shooting distance. A *jacal* is a building made by hammering long stakes into the ground—much like a corral—and plastering them over both inside and outside in semblance of an adobe house. It is positively not an adobe house, and not much of a house of any kind when bullets start whistling through. For the stakes are set at least two inches apart and wet mud is after all only wet mud which eventually dries and makes no sort of resistance to the product of Mr. Remington operating in the firearms of Mr. Colt.

Any likelihood of the Spanish-American population of the Upper, Middle or Lower Plaza doing anything in behalf of young Mr. Baca was spoiled by the fact that the greater part of the populace was suffering from that malignant affliction known as yellow jaundice.

Included in the number so affected were the male members of the community who had in the past enjoyed considerable Indian war experience and might have been willing to relieve the pressure on Baca by stray pot shots in the direction of the invading Texans.

It was the practice of the invaders to do their artillery work in volume. It was not a question of one shot following another at intervals, but of one concerted volley directed full into the *jacal*—pronounced hack-awl. In the circumstances young Baca was resigned to fate. He did what he could in protection, which was practically nothing at all, and sat down in a corner of the hut to await the end. He retained interest in the proceedings, however, to the point of watching carefully through the cracks in the weary structure for possible views of a Texas head that might be started on its way to eternity. All told in the battle he made way with four more or less prominent Texas citizens, and wounded others, who did not boast about it when it was all over.

The day dragged slowly for young Elfego. In the *jacal* he found a plaster paris reproduction of a saint, known as *Mi Senora Santa Ana*. Upon the head of the worthy saint, young Baca was wont to rest his Stetson hat in such a position as to be evident through the tiny windows of the hut to the impatient Texans. His own position would be in another part of the fort. Attempts to take Baca by surprise were met by well aimed shots that discouraged them. To make things more difficult for the imprisoned young man, the cowboys stretched blankets between the houses where they were located. It gave Baca nothing to fire at, and it gave the Slaughter troupe a splendid vantage point for attack.

The concerted firing was kept up and the *jacal* was becoming more riddled by the minute. Along about six o'clock of the first day, a barrage of shots cut away the stakes that made up the construction of the *jacal* and deposited a section of the building upon the form of young Baca. He was pinned by falling debris, pushed over on his face with his legs firmly held from behind by heaps of mortar and falling stakes. He lay in this position for a period of two hours without attempting to free himself and quite content to listen to the "Swoosh!" of the bullets over his head. Upon arrival of darkness, he pulled himself from his crouching position and took stock of his chances. He decided upon due deliberation that it mattered very little what he did. Since life was to remain but little longer within his sturdy frame, he decided that it was as well to act at home in his refuge. The hot stove—left by the departing owner—was still alive. He put on additional sticks of cottonwood, and brought it to a fine blaze. He made coffee; he heated meat; and he made—last but by far not least—he made *tortillas!* But, as Mr. Baca was honest enough to admit forty years later, he was not hungry in the slightest, and his mastication was only perfunctory—a sort of culinary defiance of the fates. He was not hungry then and he was not hungry in the morning twenty-four hours after his confinement when he employed the stove again for preparation of breakfast.

Near midnight of the first night, Baca from his place of hiding saw a tiny light creeping along the ground in his direction. He was not aware of it—having at the time no knowledge of mining such as he was later to have—but what was approaching him was a lighted fuse attached to a stick of dynamite which had been secured from the Cooney mining comp by sundry of Slaughter's cowboys who had galloped off in that direction

when it was once evident that young Elfego was
not to be dislodged from his refuge without the
demise of many.

"I saw the light," relates Mr. Baca, forty
years later, "but thought it was a cigarette butt
thrown by one of the cowboys and being blown in
my direction by the wind. I watched it curiously.
It would be still for a moment and then it would
come on again. I thought it was funny that a
cigarette should keep lit that long, but I didn't
know any other explanation of it. I didn't know
what dynamite or a fuse was at that time. The
light kept coming and I kept watching and the
next thing I know: BLOOEY!!!!"

Plaster fell in all directions and half of the
jacal collapsed in ruins. With the luck that remained with him always, the half that collapsed
was not the half that held Elfego. What remained
of the *jacal* after the previous shower of bullets
and now the shattering of the dynamite was one
protected corner where Baca stood.

Dynamite or no dynamite the followers of
Slaughter by this time had such an opinion of the
charmed existence of young Baca that they re-
frained from investigating the result of their
night's work until morning.

At the first bright peeps of dawn, they looked
anxiously in the direction of the temporary abode
of Mr. Baca. What their astonished eyes beheld
was a tiny trickle of smoke coming from the chim-

ney in the lone remaining section of the house. Mr.
Baca was having breakfast! And the fervent
Texas curses threatened to dry up the Frisco with
their vehemence. There was simply no dealing
with a fellow as lucky as that! They took out
their wrath in successive and vindictive volleys
that hit every last remaining individual thing in
the *jacal* except the form of one Baca. At the
trial was exhibited a broom with eight bullet holes
in the handle. The door of the hut—about half
the size of an ordinary door of these days—contained 367 bullet holes and had all the appearance
of a first-class sieve. It was testified that over
4,000 bullets penetrated the *jacal* when the fusillade finally ceased at 6 o'clock on the evening of
the second day. In other words, Elfego Baca held
off the eighty Texans from 9 o'clock of one morning until 6 o'clock of the next evening—a total of
33 hours.

But on the morning of the second day, the
Slaughter outfit was far from calling a truce.
They concentrated steady fire on the lone corner
of the *jacal* still remaining until it seemed impossible for human form to keep alive in the hurri-
cane. Everything was hit but Elfego Baca.
Spoons and knives and forks—all came in for
their individual attention by the pistol adeptness
of the Texans, but Elfego was untouched.

About ten o'clock, Baca saw a form start
across the open space between the blankets of the

Slaughter outfit and the hut wherein he stood. It was a cowboy sheltered behind the cast-iron front of what had once been a stove. He kept well covered and he approached slowly and with care. Nothing showed above the cast-iron surface. The figure had all the appearance of a knight of old accoutred for the joust but minus the horse. The armour was home-made but highly effective. Elfego wasted no shots. He watched with a hawk-like eye for the first slip-up of the armoured Texan. He watched for the first mistake in the slow business-like crawl; he watched for the first er-rored appearance of the cowboy's head over the top of the rejuvenated stove. With patience his chance came. There *was* a fleeting second when the cowboy's discretion was not equal to his valor. He ventured a peek at his goal. It was his last peek of the day. The bullet from Elfego's gun entered his scalp and journeyed across the top of his pate and skimmed off into space. It was as lovely a shot as ever made by Annie Oakley in her palmy days. It was a perfect shot. It put an end to progress toward the present residence of El-fego Baca by way of cast-iron aid. The cowboy was not dead—indeed, very far from dead, but he had enough for the day. He bore his bleeding scalp hastily back to the protection of his fellows.

With four dead and many more wounded, the Slaughter outfit took pause to consider the mat-ter. Mr. Cook goes on from here to say that:

The statuette of *Mi Senora Santa Ana* which Elfego used in the *jacal* to fool the Texans, and which is still worshipped as a good luck omen.

"Excitement ran high. Baca must be killed or captured. Just how either was to be effected was a question. Many plans were suggested. By this time everyone was convinced that Baca would sell his life as dearly as possible. He was at bay and thoroughly aroused. A number of my English friends were with me in the Plaza. I told them that I considered the Americans gathered at the Plaza neither more nor less than a mob. Baca, I was informed, was a county officer, and the law was on his side. I felt that although he may have overdone his duty, the best thing possible for all concerned was not to kill him, but to secure him and get him to the County Seat at Socorro."

It was very good of Mr. Cook to be so considerate of Elfego Baca, who had so far done rather well in defending himself. It would seem, offhand, that sympathy was rather due the Texas cowboys who had been most unconscionably handled by the lone Baca in a ruined hut. It was also true, however, and must be admitted, that there would be a time when Baca would have to surrender. Cook's effort at compromise was something that Baca had cause to be thankful for.

Mr. Cook writes further: "An American deputy sheriff named Ross put in appearance about this time; but he did not care to take a chance by showing himself to Baca in order to talk to him and persuade him to come out of the fort."

Mr. Ross may have subsequently amounted to

very little in an historical way, but he should at least have mention here as a gentleman of rare good sense. He did later go into the Plaza toward the *jacal* with intent at mollification and compromise with the doughty young Baca, but he went in company with Cook and a Spanish-American friend of Baca's named Francisquito Naranjo. "A very brave man," says Mr. Baca forty years later in speaking of Mr. Naranjo, "and my good friend".

It was Cook who took it upon himself to recruit Naranjo from the group of Spanish-Americans who were now gathered in numbers about the Plaza on the hills that skirted the river valley. Cook went up to address the Spanish-Americans, making them the proposition that he and Ross should go unarmed into the space in the Plaza before the *jacal* with someone whose voice Baca would recognize and listen to—provided he was still alive. "The evidence showed," writes Cook, "that four thousand shots had been fired into the *jacal* in which Baca had been hiding since he had killed Herne." Cook, as has been said, had conversed with the Spanish-American friends of Baca. "I told the Mexicans," writes Cook further, "that if Baca were alive and would give himself up, I would be responsible to them for his life until he could be taken to the county seat. To my surprise, my offer was agreed to."

Mr. Cook surely had little need for surprise.

Naranjo, as a mean manipulator of a gun himself and as a close friend of Elfego Baca, was fully aware of the slim chance his pal would have for life the longer the battle went on. He was more than anxious to risk a shot from Elfego for the chance of getting him out of the *jacal* alive and to the protection of the county jail at Socorro. He came down into the Plaza with Cook and Ross, and once within hailing distance of the hut, called to Baca: "Are you alive? Come on out; you're well protected!"

Baca was startled out of his wits, both by the nearness of the voice that had approached that close without his knowing it, and by the fact that it was the voice of his friend, Naranjo.

"Naranjo!" he yelled, "is it you?"

"*Si,*" bellowed Naranjo in return. "It's all right. Come on out!"

Suddenly, according to the report of Cook, Baca sprang out of the *jacal* through a small window opening. He had, says Cook, a six shooter in each hand, and was clad only in his under clothes. This is a quaint touch which Elfego, forty years later, denies vehemently. It is a matter of small moment. It is enough to know that Baca descended suddenly into the sunlight of the Plaza by way of a small window opening in the hut.

From where he had been in the fort, he could not see the party of which Naranjo was one, and when he alighted and saw Cook and Ross he felt immediately that he had been double crossed by his friend. He was still afire with the certainty that he was going to stay alive as long as the fates were willing.

"Line up!" he yelled sharply to Cook and Ross, flourishing the two guns menacingly and maneuvering the Americans between himself and the cowboys across the Plaza. Cook and Ross remembering the incident of the "one, two, three, BANG!" wasted no time in obeying orders. Ross and Cook were in a perilous position, for they knew that a false move would bring the Baca guns into action. Baca was also in a bad fix, for his friends from the hillside in the excess of their enthusiasm at seeing him alive, yelled for him to make a run for it. Plain suicide could not compare in certainty with a run then with rifles in the hands of the best shots in New Mexico trained upon him from the first break.

As it was, things were again getting dark for Baca. The Texans were crowding in on him from their hiding places on three sides of the Plaza, and there was insistence that the dirty Mexican be hanged *pronto.* Cook, as the arranger of the compromise and with the gun of Baca aimed at his breast, made a very hasty and highly creditable speech to the effect that they all knew how Baca had been induced to surrender, and that it would mean death to him, (Cook), either immediately or later, if Baca were not given safe escort to Socorro.

"Immediately," said Baca, to reassure him.

Cook's talk, as he reports it, did not seem to satisfy either his Texas friends or his new acquaintance, Mr. Baca. He concludes forty years later that his death then would not have interfered greatly with the happiness of the Slaughter Cohorts, so he talked to them in a different vein. He told them that they were a mob in the eyes of the law; that Baca had done things for which he could not escape being hanged; and that the laws of the land, not a mob, should attend to his case. He also reminded them—which was more effective —that any double dealing with Baca would result in a pretty little race war indulged in by half the State of New Mexico and which would end in the eventual decease of all of them—if they remained to do business in the vicinity. They considered that carefully and agreed that the escort would be afforded Mr. Baca upon his complete surrender. All he had to do was to give up his guns and place himself in the hands of the jolly Slaughter boys for the trip to Socorro.

Would Mr. Baca give up his guns! Mr. Baca would as soon leap off the rim of the Grand Canyon on the back of a giraffe. Mr. Baca's guns would leave his hands only after life had grown cold within him. Mr. Baca would go to Socorro on one condition only. That was that he was to

retain full use of his two guns, and that he was to
be allowed to sit on the rear seat of a buck board
wagon with the Slaughter troup entire before him.
Ross, the deputy, was to sit in the front seat of
the buck board with the driver, and Baca was to
be in the rear of all of them during the trip to
Socorro.

The cavalcade started the long ride to Socorro
that took all of the night and the better part of
the next day. Baca arrived in Socorro a hero, but
also a captive. He was locked up in the new county jail. The new jail sat almost exactly upon the
precise spot where Elfego Baca was born. The
jail was barely finished in time to receive Baca,
the first prisoner. The first case tried in the new
court house was of the same Elfego Baca, arising
out of the Frisco riot. It was only one of the small
coincidences that make life so interesting.

In concluding the Frisco incident, Mr. Cook
writes: ''I left New Mexico a short time after
the trouble at the San Francisco Plaza, and never
knew the outcome of Baca's trial until within the
last few years, when I learned that he was not
hanged for the shooting of those men in the Plaza.
On the contrary he had become one of the most
prominent attorneys in the State of New Mexico.
Should Mr. Baca read about this incident, the part
which I played in it, and my point of view about
the affair, I think he will readily understand why
I have reason to be very glad that no greater loss

of life was caused by Cowboy McCarty's efforts
to work off a little surplus energy in an attempt
to terrorize a peaceful Mexican settlement.''

Elfego Baca was tried twice for the Frisco
killings, and acquitted on both charges. They are
among the famous trials of New Mexico. Prose-
cuting Baca were H. B. Fergusson, district attorney and later representative to Congress from
New Mexico; Colonel Brethen and Neill B. Field.
He was defended by Attorney Shaw, Judge Warrant and B. S. Rodey, later federal judge in both
Porto Rico and Alaska and representative to congress.

Not the least interesting part of the testimony
was that of a cowboy who testified solemnly and
with utmost seriousness that if he took a .45 Colt
pistol, aimed it directly at Baca's chest from a
distance of a foot away, and fired,—there would
be absolutely no effect. He gave it as his deliber-
ate opinion that Elfego was possessed of something from God or the devil, and that he would
not be surprised if it were a great deal more from
the latter than from the former.

It is this same legend of a ''charmed exist-
ance'' that made the little plaster saint of St.
Anna so cherished a possession of the Spanish-
American family who rescued it from the ruins of
the *jacal* and, though very poor and needy, refused
subsequently to part with it. Proper ceremonies
are celebrated every Saint Anna's day in the sec-

tion about Magdalena where the plaster saint now resides.

It is worshipped as a good luck emblem, and Elfego's own offer of ten cows for the plaster image was respectfully turned down. There can be no price for a saint that was responsible for the miracle of the Middle Plaza at the village of San Francisco.

CHAPTER FOUR

Elfego Plays Robin Hood at Kelly

It was necessary that there should be a comic interlude following the long aftermath of the Frisco trouble. It was furnished by Elfego's cousin, Conrado Baca, who operated a combined store and saloon in partnership with one Frank Shaw in the little mining town of Kelly.

The miners and cowboys of the Kelly neighborhood were of the same jolly, rough nature made famous by the Slaughter clan and numerous other wandering and romantic tribes of bronco busters who have come down to us through Buffalo Bill and the later Tom Mix and Buck Jones of the silver sheet. They were gay and a bit free with their six guns, but their hearts were in the right place. They were broken to the habit of making the Baca and Shaw store a shooting gallery on Saturday nights. They could practice target shooting on the skillets that hung in profusion from the rafters of the emporium, and when skillets palled on them, they could always supplement the excitement by striving manfully to separate the buttons from the coats of Mr. Baca or Mr. Shaw at the considerable distance of twenty or thirty paces.

In the interests of good merchandising, Mr.

Conrado Baca and Mr. Frank Shaw bore with this for long weeks. But there came a Saturday night when patience ceased to be a Sunday school virtue. It was the night when Mr. Conrado Baca underwent the stirring experience of having, simultaneously, two buttons clipped neatly from the vest that covered his bosom, the while his hat was being lifted expertly from his thatch by another bullet and the buckle of his belt was being polished by a fourth. It was then that Mr. Conrado Baca and Mr. Frank Shaw decided that the marts of trade could struggle along without their efforts until armed help should arrive in their support. They lit out over the hills for Socorro in search of the cousin of Conrado, by name Elfego.

They found Elfego Baca, resting on his laurels from the Frisco fight, and not uneager to be drafted anew in the cause of justice. He agreed willingly to proceed to Kelly and see what the hell went on there. Did Mr. Conrado Baca and Mr. Shaw desire to return with Mr. Elfego Baca to Kelly to see that their interests were protected? No, if it were all the same to Mr. Elfego Baca, they should prefer to remain in Socorro until peace arrived in Kelly.

Elfego hopped his pony and headed for Kelly, which had a fine free name in those wild mining days, with two saloons and three houses of ill repute for every private residence. Kelly was but fifteen miles from Socorro and Elfego arrived there the evening after the departure of his cousin, Conrado. He found the store in possession of various energetic, care-free cowpunchers and miners.

"What's this?" said Elfego in a loud voice, as he entered the store.

"What's what?" said the hard-boiled babies from the range, pushing their countenances in the direction of Elfego, and dragging forth a rapid gun to point the humor of their interrogation. They were, however, a trifle late, and were quite content to forego the pleasure of range practice for the benefit of getting their hands in the air rapidly enough to satisfy the burly young Spanish-American who was covering them.

"What's this?" said Elfego calmly. "What do you mean by taking possession of this here store. You know it doesn't belong to you, don't you?"

"Who the hell are you?" asked a gentleman with less than ordinary regard for the sight of the next morn.

"I", said Elfego modestly, "I am Elfego Baca."

The west of then was not the west of now, but news had a way of traveling even before the advent of the radio. Much like the radio in fact, scurrying about from ranch to ranch in a way no modern newspaper, no modern invention is ever likely to emulate. Elfego Baca was known wherever a Colt pistol had any authority in New Mexico.

"Elfego Baca!" said the bold spirit, dropping his hands in disgust. "Why the hell didn't you say so! Who wants the old dump? We was just keepin' it for 'em till they got back."

There was instant amiability on all hands, followed by a drink from the bar run by Baca and Shaw in connection with their store. The emporium was turned over to Mr. Baca with the best wishes of his new found friends.

The new responsibility irked Elfego almost immediately. He was not a store-keeper, had no wish to be a store-keeper, and had almost total disregard for such store-keepers as Conrado and Shaw, who would let themselves be frightened away from their own business. It was a thriving business, with an estimated stock of $3,500. Elfego had ideas of what a store-keeper should be, and Conrado and Shaw did not in the slightest conform to his notion of a merchant prince. In simple, so Elfego's mind ran, if Conrado and Shaw didn't think enough of their business to fight for it they didn't deserve to have a business. He acted upon this philosophy at once.

He sent word by eager messengers to the tiny Mexican *jacals* of the neighborhood that tomorrow morning was going to be one of the red letter days of Socorro County, one of the great moments in the life of Kelly and vicinity. In short, the famous Elfego Baca would, next morning promptly at nine o'clock, begin dispensing the merchandise of the store of Baca and Shaw to the native population of Kelly free of charge, first come, first served, and might the devil take the hindmost.

So ordered, so done. At nine o'clock, Elfego and associates successfully gave away every last bit of merchandise on the shelves of Baca and Shaw. It was a bag of flour to this astonished native of Spanish decent (Oh, marvelous Elfego Baca!); half a dozen cans of beans to this repre- sentative of the Chaves or Otero or Romero family (Oh, most benignant Elfego Baca!); a slab of bacon to this poor sample of the early *Conquistadores* (Oh, most beneficent Elfego Baca!). It was a momentous occasion, it was Robin Hood done in Spanish.

The merchandise of solid hue out of the way, Elfego turned to the disposal of the liquid stock of Baca and Shaw. This was done with even greater ease through the assistance of the drivers of the eight-horse ore teams that laboriously drag- ged the product of the Kelly mines into Socorro. Would the drivers of the Kelly mine teams have a drink—a free for nothing, entirely gratis drink? WOULD the drivers of the Kelly mine teams have a free, gratis drink! Gentlemen, step back from in front of the door or prepare to be trampled in the rush!

The hauling of valuable ore from Kelly to

Socorro practically ceased on that celebrated day.

Whether Mr. Elfego Baca was astute enough to foresee the wonderful effect the action at Kelly would have on the susceptible voters of Socorro County should he ever present himself for their favors, is a question virtually insoluble at this late day, but it is not too far from probability to assume that it did no harm to the gentleman's chances when the occasion arose.

Mr. Conrado Baca and Mr. Shaw, waiting half joyfully, half apprehensively at Socorro for tidings of the restoration of their cherished property received a shock comparable to the Fall of the Bastille when the first incomplete returns began coming in from the country precincts. What harsher form of hysteria they went through as the complete vote was tabulated can be left to the imagination of the most dull. They desired ardently to have immediate confab with Mr. Elfego Baca, but there was not in them—despite travail almost insupportable—the courage necessary to descend upon Kelly and wait upon the gentleman. They waited instead—very impatiently, be it supposed—in Socorro, and welcomed Elfego upon his return with tearful eyes, mild but anguished remonstrances, and a deal of beseeching.

There was really no moral or legal excuse for the action of Mr. Elfego Baca in the case, but there was a strong romantic appeal in what he did. He wasted but a few minutes in repeating to them his reasoning of a few days before; to-wit, that they had no right to property they couldn't protect. There was no use in restoring their rights now if they were only to lose them again at the first shot. He made no mention of the possibility that Messrs. Baca and Shaw might have saved something from the wreckage by selling out their stock and leaving Kelly to its fate. He made no mention of the possibility because it had doubtless never occurred to him. New Mexico was, in those days, an incurably romantic State, and it seemed perfectly proper to Elfego Baca that he should make assignment of the property of Mr. Shaw and his cousin in the way he thought best fitted to its disposal. Messrs. Baca and Shaw seemed unfitted to manage their affairs, and were willing to depart them for a place of safety. The good citizenry of Kelly and surroundings were more than thankful for the Gentleman Bountiful who had made their existence full for at least one day in a hard life.

This being the case, what was there to holler about? Did Messrs. Baca and Shaw desire to holler? Mr. Elfego Baca fixed them with a piercing eye. Messrs. Baca and Shaw disclaimed any intention of hollering. They just wanted to know what it was all about. Since it was done as it had been done, why, of course . . . . Adios, Elfego. See you again soon!

CHAPTER FIVE

THE LYNCHING OF JOE FOWLER

The reluctance of Elfego to submit to the gentle caresses of the Clan Slaughter at Frisco was due in greater or less part to the sudden end of Joe Fowler, who, several years before, had been lynched by the Vigilantes of Socorro, masquerading as the state militia. A mob of armed men in an agitated condition was not the proper playmate for a young man desiring prolonged existence.

Joe Fowler was a prominent killer of the Southwest in the days when there was considerable distinction to the honor and keen competition. There are several schools of thought in regard to Mr. Fowler. One is to the effect that Fowler was a dirty this and that who would as soon shoot a man as look at him, and who had a habit of settling up his little bills payable to cowpunchers who had worked for him by bumping them off on pay day and disposing of the remains. What with rustling most of his cattle to start with and paying his help only one tiny bullet on pay day, the Fowler overhead was practically nil. This, we remind you, is the report of only one scientific committee.

The other is just as vehement in stating that though Joe Fowler was a rough cookie and a bit

Elfego Baca at the age of 18, shortly after the Frisco episode.

too free with a weapon when a few shots of *tiquila* were swishing dangerously around within him, he was at heart a well-meaning, well-behaved fellow who had considerable business ability and a very nice ranch property.

There is, as you see, confusion up to this point. From here on the case of Joe Fowler gets a bit clearer. It is well established that on a certain day about the time we are speaking of, Fowler arrived in Socorro in company with Mrs. Fowler and bearing about his person the sum of $25,000 which was half payment for the sale of his ranch. Mr. Fowler was entitled by all laws of heaven and at least that part of the earth that housed New Mexico to show proper elation over this good fortune. He did so by encasing within himself a fair portion of the liquid refreshments of divers and sundry bars of the good, lively town of Socorro.

With this load aboard, Fowler started to attend to a few of the pressing things that had brought him to town. He went first of all to the office of Socorro's only newspaper, the Socorro Chieftain. The editor, knowing Mr. Fowler by reputation and perceiving his condition to be bordering on that state of ecstasy known as blotto, had a very hearty, yet fearful, smile of welcome ready for Mr. Fowler. The effort was almost entirely wasted on Mr. Fowler, who was not on hand for social but for business reasons.

"Is this," said Mr. Fowler breasting up to
the editorial sanctum and pushing his jaw well
forward in hope of contradiction, "is this the
damned noospaper?"

The editor, with what he hoped was a smile
of utter friendship and cameraderie but which had
all the sickly appearance of a man just risen from
nine weeks of pneumonia, admitted that it was the
very same.

"Well," said Mr. Fowler weaving about in
front of the editor and a bit hazy on the proper
etiquette, "I want to put an ad in your dam
paper."

He spoke in the form of a question—a question which was answered very pronto by the editor, who pushed paper and pencil across the table
in the direction of Mr. Fowler and came hastily
around the table to find a chair for Mr. Fowler.
The Prince of Wales in all his travels has never
received such instant and spontaneous apprecia-
tion.

Mr. Fowler unleashed his handiest gun, laid
it carefully on the table before him and sat down
to serious composition. Be it said at once that
Mr. Fowler shot better than he wrote. The pen
may be mightier than the Colt, but not in the hands
of Joe Fowler. His fingers seemed overly thick
for fluent chirography and his tongue was in
danger of complete collapse by. the time he stop-

ped rolling it and got the last of the few necessary words down on paper.

He arose, gave his gun a pleasurable twirl
as if in joyous release from the burdens of author-
ship, and tossed the paper across the table to the
editor.

"Here," he said, "put this in yer damned
noospaper."

It was accompanied by a ten dollar gold piece,
and a grand manner. Mr. Fowler gathered up his
overloaded body and withdrew from the scene.

The editor, waiting carefully until Mr. Fowler was entirely out of sight, made bold to read the
communication that was to feature his sheet for
the coming week. It ran:

"I hev muny to pay my detts. Eny blankety
blank (our words, not Mr. Fowler's) I owe kin
kum and git it.

JOE FOWLER."

Mr. Fowler proceeded down the street until
he came to the saloon of Mr. Bob Monroe known
as the Windsor Hotel. The exercise in pedestrianism had whetted his whistle to the point
where additional refreshments were necessary.
He acquired them in company with "friends" who
knew it was just as well to be agreeable when Joe
Fowler hinted at it. They drank with Mr. Fowler
and they laughed over-loudly at his not particularly brilliant jibes. Mr. Fowler, warmed by his own
scintillation, sought to add to his pleasure by re-

quiring the terpsichorean efforts of various of his jolly chums. He brought forth two guns of weighty and deadly appearance and roared very appreciatively at the antics of the gentlemen avoiding his marksmanship. He danced them here and he danced them there, and life never seemed so full of zest for Mr. Fowler.

At the height of the frolic, Mr. Monroe, the proprietor, conceiving a fancied duty to his guests, leaned far over the counter, yanked Mr. Fowler around the neck vigorously and brought him back prostrate over the bar in a position where his bartenders could relieve Mr. Fowler of his weapons. He then released Mr. Fowler with his regrets. That gentleman wasted a few moments in recovering his lost breath, and then, with the subtlety of the wicked, grinned amiably at his own foolishness and walked along the bar toward the proprietor in the friendliest of manners.

Once opposite the proprietor, he wheeled suddenly with an opened clasp knife in his hand and neatly cut out half the heart of that gentleman with one deft jab of the weapon.

There is here again dispute as to just what happened following the slaying of the hotel man. Some have it that Fowler secured guns, barricaded himself in the second story of the hotel and only gave himself up days later when friends promised him a safe cell and a fair trial. Less romantic accounts are to the effect that Fowler was dragged off to the hoosegow forthwith and without ceremony.

Be that as it may, the trial of Fowler was of a spectacular nature. Armed with the $25,000 from the sale of his ranch he was able to secure the best legal talent in his behalf. His misfortune lay in the fact that previous gun pleasures in Socorro County had resulted in the formation of the Socorro Vigilantes, who had little or no compunction in stringing up such a character as Joe Fowler or any other who sought to make of Socorro their private shooting gallery.

The trial was held in the old court house at Socorro, in an exceptionally large, low, adobe court room with many window seats. In each of these window seats sat representatives of the Vigilantes with their guns hidden not the slightest out of any respect for the majesty of the law. The guns for the most part were trained on Mr. Fowler, who sat defiantly in a chair which was nailed to the floor. Around the nether limbs of Fowler rested several of the heaviest, most dominating shackles and balls of lead ever seen in an American court. In the atmosphere of the court, Fowler really had little chance. The jury was selected, the evidence was taken, and the jury returned with a verdict of guilty in the first degree.

Fowler languished in jail. There were constant rumors of the approach of an armed band from Texas to release Fowler from the tedium of

penal servitude and take a few whacks at the
Socorro citizenry in the process. There was also
rumor of appeal to the territorial supreme court,
and the Vigilantes were just as heatedly opposed
to this. It has been said that Mrs. Fowler hired
sundry handy men with the gun to loiter as closely under the window of her husband's cell as possible with a view of despatching from this life anyone so brash as to attempt anything detrimental
to his welfare.

There were strings pulled here and strings
pulled there, and very few strings pulled on behalf of Fowler. The fear of the Texas raid and
of the slow and tortuous workings of the law that
might result in Fowler's escaping the noose,
caused pressure to be brought to bear in high
places. The pressure finally resulted in an order
from the territorial governor to the sheriff of
Socorro County that the person of one Joseph
Fowler should be turned over to Company something or other of state milita for "safe keeping".

The majestic irony of this has perhaps never
been equalled on sea or land. The assumption was
that the sheriff and the friends of Fowler were
not capable of looking after his interests, but that
the company of state militia stationed at Socorro
was. The state militia at Socorro, it may as well
be admitted at once, was made up almost exclus-
ively of the Vigilantes of Socorro. The malignant
helpfulness of the Governor of the territory of

New Mexico meant only one thing to the citizens of Socorro. It meant the sudden end of Joe Fowler.

Mr. Fowler's attorney brought the news to him in the jail.

"They're going to hang you tonight, Joe," he said frankly.

Fowler looked at him earnestly and eagerly.

"Mr. Lawyer," he said, "if you could smuggle a couple of guns into me here, I'd be mighty obliged to you. Could you do that, Mr. Lawyer? I certainly would be obliged to you." Mr. Fowler was all eagerness.

But there was no chance of getting guns to Fowler, even if the lawyer had been disposed. Joe Fowler was taken out of jail and hanged that night.

It was the knowledge of this fresh in his mind that had prompted young Elfego Baca to be careful of his friendships during and following the Frisco episode.

CHAPTER SIX

Mr. Hardcastle of England Reminisces

The author might be pardoned at this juncture for presuming to offer some observations on the pleasure of writing the biography of a living man. There might as well be reasonable interest in the slight unpleasantries likely to arise in the compiling of life of a man so active with the six shooter as Mr. Baca has been, but we are happy to disappoint you. Nothing has developed except the kindliest of relations. However, it must be admitted that Mr. Baca has not had the doubtful pleasure of seeing this manuscript of his life and will not until it appears in book form. At that time a journey may be needed, and although we are fond of travel, we can imagine trips starting under more auspicious circumstances.

This is all vaguely preliminary to saying that during the writing of this book we received a letter from Mr. Alfred Hardcastle, High Field, Hawkhurst, Kent, England. It was pure coincidence that Mr. Hardcastle, an entire stranger to us, should have written just at that time. He wrote in another connection, but he mentioned that he had lived in the Socorro district about the time of the earlier Baca episodes. With the eagerness of a true biographer we dispatched an epistle to Mr.

Hardcastle forthwith. His answer, much to the point, revealed that Mr. Hardcastle had not only taken part in the famous Frisco fight in which Elfego had held off the Texas cowboys, but had been present at the recovery of the body of Joe Fowler. We are happy to employ parts of Mr. Hardcastle's letters here in helping to substantiate our own story and in assisting, if possible, in making that hectic period more reasonable, more sensible.

Mr. Hardcastle was one of many young Englishmen who owned or helped operate New Mexico ranches in that far off day. The practise, for some reason we have not taken the trouble to ascertain, has practically died out, and it is a sad thing for New Mexico and for all of us. There is the case of the Wyoming rancher who has but lately returned to become Earl of Something or Other, but we are afraid that the instances of English interest in our ranches are becoming all too few.

"I remember an Elfego Baca," wrote Mr. Hardcastle in his second letter, "but very likely not the same as you have in mind. Socorro was full of Bacas, with old Don Luis their chieftain, and Elfego was not an uncommon name among Mexicans. The one I remember was the cause of a curious warfare lasting several days on the Frisco plaza, round Milligan's store. It was quite

an interesting story. I was "among those present." I think it was 1884.

"I won't go into the details of how it came
about, but there were two deaths of cowmen—one
named Perman whose horse was shot and fell on
hom, injuring him internally; the other named
Hearne, a very good young cowpuncher who
worked for the Spur outfit and was liked by everybody.

"An inquest was held on him in Milligan's
store and I shall never forget it, as I think the
part I played was unique in legal proceedings. I
think Milligan was elected coroner. Ned Upcher
was clerk of court. I was elected foreman of the
jury, and sat on the end of the bench, which, with
sundry boxes and flour sacks, constituted the jury
box. But—and this I believe is the unique part—
I was also called as the principal witness! At the
time of the trouble I had only been a short distance away and saw a shot fired through the door
of the little Mexican log shack, and Hearne, who
with two others was about to open the door, fell
to the ground. I was also present at his subsequent death in the back of Milligan's store.

"Anyway, I was called up from my seat on
the jury to give this evidence, and having given it
I returned to my position as foreman of the jury!
Incidentally I may mention that the result of the
inquest was that this Elfego Baca was found
guilty of murder in the first degree and con-

demned to death by the coroner—which is a climax
hardly to be expected at an inquest!

"Following this was a sort of inter-racial
warfare for a few days, which I don't think resulted in any more fatalities, and Elfego Baca was
eventually handed over to a deputy sheriff who
happened to be going through the country with a
buckboard. I don't think it can be the same Elfego Baca you know, but if it is he probably never
knew how near he was to being hung at the "Point
of Timber"—i. e., between the head of the Tula-
rosa and the San Augustine Plains. It had been
arranged that the buckboard containing the deputy sheriff, the prisoner and the guard, on their
way to Socorro, should be held up at this spot and
the hanging take place. Owing to a mistake on
the part of the Spur outfit and the JONS boys,
each thinking the other was going to do it, there
was no turned up at the trysting place, and so
the Elfego Baca of that episode may be alive now
for all I know."

Very much alive, indeed, and not a little indignant after reading Mr. Hardcastle's letter. It
would have done the heart good of any lover of
biography to have been present and heard the
snorts of Mr. Baca. It was a sight which out of
all justice should not be retained for the sole grat-
ification of the biographer. It is because of this
we mention it. Mr. Baca pointed out anew that
Hearne was not a nice cowpuncher, but was a bul-

ly with a price on his head. He knew quite well
of the lynching plot, and laughed immoderately at
the idea it failed because of mixed signals. It
failed, said Mr. Baca more than a trifle testily, at
the behest of the deputy sheriff who knew he
would be a moribund as a flounder the instant anybody showed up and made a gesture toward the
person of Elfego Baca, who sat in the back seat
and fondled his weapons.

The mails between New Mexico and England
are not of the speediest, but in due course we received from Mr. Hardcastle word that he could do
nothing but reiterate the statements he had already made, and from Mr. Baca—upon bringing
the matter to his attention—we had word that he
could do nothing but reiterate the statements HE
had made. It was not a controversy, and we
should not like to have it considered in that light.
It is, obviously, asking too much for opponents—
even friendly ones after a lapse of forty years—
to see every last incident with an eye single. It is
enough to know that the main facts are corrobor-
ated from more than a single source.

You will recall the meeting with Mr. George
Ade, proprietor of the Los Lunas hotel, and his
corroboration of the main physical incidents of
the escape of Baca *Pere* from the Los Lunas jail.
We have now to report added incidents in the
famous case of Joe Fowler. The most important
ones are furnished by Mr. Hardcastle, but the

most startling ones came from another source. We shall get to that in a few minutes. First let us hear the highly interesting story of Mr. Hard-castle.

"You say you have been writing an account of Joe Fowler. No doubt you have much material concerning that malefactor. I arrived at the Grand Central hotel, Socorro, November 1883, the day after he had stabbed a man in the hotel and was arrested and put in the jail. I was told the hotel was full up except for one little room, of which the floor was still very wet as they had been cleaning it. I said that made no difference, but I also found the bed seemed very damp. It was not till the next day that I learned that this was the room the poor stabbed man was put into and where he died during the night.

"It was about a year after I think, in the winter, that I again happened to be in Socorro, and that night was sitting around the big iron stove in the "office" of the Grand Central to-gether with a few friends. We were smoking and "swapping lies" 'till long after everybody had gone to bed. Around the stove were Pete Simp-son, the sheriff, and Billy Minters, the well known and highly esteemed "gentleman gambler" (as he was called as opposed to the "tin horn" fra-ternity). After midnight the most scared man I ever saw dashed in to find Pete Simpson. He had a Winchester in his hand, and stammered out with his teeth chattering: 'They've taken *Joe* out!'

"This caused Pete Simpson to be slightly less agitated than would have seemed proper. Apparently he was not entirely taken by surprise, as this messenger was one of a party of extra guards which had been placed in the jail that night. Joe had managed to obtain fresh trials and postponement of sentence for a year, and just at that time had been granted another trial and a change of venue. This meant that the following day he was going to Santa Fe, there to be tried again. The citizens of Socorro got wind of this and determined to end the Joe Fowler business then and there. The "Vigilantes" accordingly forced an entrance into the jail and dragged Joe out and duly carried out the sentence of "Judge Lynch".

"On receiving the message of the terrified special guard, Pete Simpson consulted with us around the stove and decided the correct procedure would be for him, accompanied by a few "good men and true", to go at the first streak of day to the fatal spot and cut Joe down. Billy Minters, another man I cannot remember, and I volunteered to go with him.

"It was bitterly cold when we started out. We proceeded along 'Death Alley' which was a lane running along the south side of the town, and so called because it had, on several previous occasions, been the scene of similar episodes. As dawn began to show we saw Socorro mountain straight ahead covered with snow. It formed a background against which we saw silhouetted with sharp distinctness a human form clad in black apparently standing in air. It was not light enough to see the rope until we got quite close. There was an adobe wall running all along Death Alley on the left hand side, and cottonwoods growing along at intervals.

"One of the cottonwoods had been selected as especially suitable, as it had a strong projecting limb and the victim could be put up on the wall and then, with the noose adjusted, pushed off into eternity. Se we found Joe. He was dressed in his best black suit, his boots shined up, his face shaved and his mustache waxed out. His big black Stetson was on the road immediately below his feet, there placed according to the strict etiquette of Judge Lynch.

"I remember thinking that early morning that I had never known anything that gave the impression of bitter desolate cold as did that break of day, in that dreary Death Alley with the snow-clad Socorro mountains facing us and that cold grey hanging corpse in its black apparel. Pete Simpson, the sheriff, sprang a point of law on us to the effect that the body could not be cut down without a Justice of the Peace present. This surprising legal point may have existed only in Pete's imagination. None of us except Pete knew where to find a Justice, but just at that moment there appeared from nowhere a semi-drunk man, not yet recovered from his booze of the previous night. A kind of no-good-for-anything saloon 'bum' such as Socorro had plenty of. He was commandeered to fetch the Justice of the Peace, and after some delay they arrived in a one-horse buggy. The J. P. seemed surprised that his consent was required, but promptly gave it, and Joe was lowered to the ground. By that time a big hefty nigger had appeared and he volunteered to drive Joe back to town, a job which no one else seemed to hanker for. Joe was boosted up and seated beside the nigger and looked gruesomely like a live person sitting there.

"The buggy started off, but at the first jolt of the rough road Joe fell down and had to be replaced. The coon then put his arm around him in a manner which looked grotesquely affectionate, and eventually drove him to the 'Texas Ed' saloon where the body 'lay in state' for the whole day, much to the profit of the bar of that saloon. It was a big saloon on the northeast corner of the Plaza and was formerly owned by Charley Utter, a little tin horn who wore his hair long, bore a chin whisker and long Prince Albert coat with considerable flashy jewelry, and flattered himself that he looked like Buffalo Bill.

"It was always a moot point why Joe Fowler had slicked himself up so finely on that last night.

Either it was in anticipation of the journey on the train to Santa Fe next day or, as many claimed, because he had an inkling the Vigilantes would take him that night, and, if the worst came to the worst, he meant to 'dress his part' as well as possible. He was said to have killed thirteen men,— not counting Mexicans! There was no record of his killings having been done otherwise than by shooting in the back or when he had the 'dead drop'. He was said to have been the originator of packing guns in especially arranged scabbards under the armpits, out of sight under his vest. But he always carried a Wells Fargo 'sawed-off' shot gun across his saddle, and with this he destroyed Butcher-Knife Bill and another cow puncher as they were cooking dinner south of the Point of Rocks just in the southeast corner of Augustine Plains at the East end of the Luera mountains. The spot was known for years after as "Rustler's Grave" and though it is more than 30 years since I last passed that way, I could ride straight to those graves now."

Things must surely run by coincidences. We shall never again scorn a writer or playwright who resorts to them. We were in the midst of reading Mr. Hardcastle's thrilling story about the end of Joe Fowler when a handsome old Spanish-American came into our office bearing a note of introduction from a friend of ours. The old gentleman spoke very broken English, and it was all of ten minutes before we got the combination of it. Then it began to dawn on us that he was telling us a story of the lynching of Joe Fowler. Not only that, but a story which sought to prove that although Joe Fowler had been lynched, the job had been a poor one and that he had left Socorro in a rough box, but very much alive! And that he had still been alive as late as 1924 in California!

There are those who say biography is a dull business! The old gentleman was very dignified and very honest appearing, and he told his story with a zeal for the exact truth which we should never attempt to doubt. He sat there before us and unfolded his story of Joe Fowler as authentically and as vividly as if it had happened yesterday instead of 40 years ago.

Joe Fowler was not dead, he declared. It was true that he had been taken from the jail at Socorro and hanged from a cottonwood. It was also true that the body had been cut down and taken to the "Texas Ed" saloon where it had remained in state all day. But it was also true that he, Jose Lucero, with his mother had gone to see Joe Fowler because they loved him. At a time when they could be alone with the body of Fowler, he, Jose, then only a young boy, had placed a mirror to the mouth of Joe Fowler and had seen with his own eyes the mist that covered the mirror thereafter, proving that Joe Fowler still lived. He had also remained close to the body of Joe Fowler when it was placed in a rough box and loaded on a train for California. Further than that his mother had later received a letter from Joe Fowler in California and had continued to hear from him up till the time of her death. In fact Jose Lucero had last had direct word from Joe Fowler in 1924.

To which Mr. Hardcastle could only answer, "Well!!!!" and let it go at that, evidently being as nunplussed and amazed as we were with Mr. Lucero sitting before us. Mr. Hardcastle later recovered his voice to the point of saying, "A man doesn't hang by the neck for six hours at night with the thermometer below zero, and subsequently play at breathing on mirrors. However, the atmosphere in the "Texas Ed" saloon that day and night when the "lying in state" took place was so full of strong breaths that any mirror on being exposed might well have become misty!"

Which, after all, is a very good answer, and one which we should not attempt to improve upon. Our only excuse for interrupting the story of Mr. Baca's life in this fashion is that it is that kind of a biography. Mr. Baca would be the last to object, and in truth he was insistent that capital be made of Mr. Hardcastle's extraordinarly vivid and fascinating story. We can only thank Mr. Hardcastle from the depth of our heart and get on with our own story. It seems apparent to us that no one who enjoys what goes before or after can have reason for complaint at Mr. Hardcastle's excellent recital. It would appear certain that no matter what one might think of our worth as a biographer, it would be impossible to deny that we were a fortunate one to obtain such assistance in the midst of our endeavors.

CHAPTER SEVEN

There are at intervals in the public prints
from the pens of men not afraid to speak out, a
protest against the practice of judges on the bench
assuming the office of castigator and final word
far in advance of Judgment Day.

The tableau is something like this, according
to reports given by the indignant:

"Have you anything to say for yourself before I sentence you to six months in jail, you dirty
bum?" says the judge leaning across his desk.

"Only that I wish you wouldn't call me a
dirty bum," says the prisoner mildly.

"It just occurs to me that a *year* in jail would
be a fairer sentence because you *are* such a dirty
bum," replies the judge, to show that he has understood the prisoner correctly.

"I still don't think you ought to call me a
dirty bum," says the foolish man before the bar.

"On third thought," says the judge, "because
you are so articulate about it and because you are
such a *dirty* bum, I think I'll make it two years."

"But—," says the prisoner.

"Three years," answers the judge.

And the game goes on until the man has

talked the better part of his natural life away. Providing that when it comes to famous last words, the judges generally have them.

That brings us now to two cases—one duly attested to and the other highly apocryphal—in which the court was left at the post in repartee. The one had to do with our hero, Mr. Elfego Baca, and the other with Mr. Wm. H. Bonney, known as Billy the Kid, and whom you may have heard something of before.

As one of a bevy, batch, bunch or whatever it is of lawyers on hand to hear the report of the grand jury in the district court of a certain judge for the counties of Socorro and Lincoln, Elfego was in a position to hear everything going on when his brother, Abdenago Baca, was ousted from the jury because of "undue influence on its members."

There had been extreme reluctance on the part of Abdenago Baca and others to bring in an indictment against a Spanish-American sheep-herder who had killed an Anglo cowpuncher in a quarrel over a horse. The horse had belonged to the "Mexican"; the "Anglo" had taken it, and had been killed in the rumpus that followed. There had been four attempts to secure an indictment against the sheepherder, and four failures. All due, said the district attorney, to the stubbornness of Abdenago and his hold on his colleagues of the jury. Accordingly, at the suggestion of the district attorney, the judges had called the jury in and discharged Abdenago. It was, according to the Baca code, much like a dishonorable discharge from the army, and Elfego Baca immediately arose to the defense of his next of kin.

"I think it very wrong," said Elfego Baca, "that a man should be thus dismissed without charges being brought against him, and without chance to defend his reputation."

"I think differently," said the judge, drawing himself up pompously and uttering his words in a tone to indicate that the Constitution would have little chance of survival if he should ever step down from the bench. "The court so orders . . . . Hum!"

"It doesn't matter a great deal to me what this court orders," said Elfego much in the same manner used by Clarence Darrow in a later court at Dayton, Tennessee. "The point is that after years of a clean, unsullied, respectable life, my brother is to be dismissed dishonorably from this grand jury without charges being brought against him and without chance to defend himself. I object very strenuously to that."

"The court—so—orders!" said the judge, icily.

"The court is a jackass,' retorted Mr. Baca in turn. "I'm not going to stand here and allow a corrupt and personally immoral judge like you . . . . ''

"Sheriff!" yelled the judge wildly. "Remove this man! Remove this man, I say!''

But there was no sheriff in sight. There was no deputy sheriff in sight. There were no court attaches in sight who cared to do that little thing known as arresting Elfego Baca when he felt he was in the right. The sheriff had discreetly disappeared at the first incendiary words. With him had gone deputies and important court functionaries, and Elfego was not arrested then and not arrested later.

Before you arise in indignation and leave the theater in disgust at the spectacle of law and order thus being thwarted, it is as well to know that the same judge was removed from office shortly after the Socorro incident as a result of pressure brought to bear in Washington because of these same personally immoral acts of the judge mentioned by Mr. Baca. The character of a judge, after all, has everything to do with the conduct of people in his court. We cease the sermon, forthwith, and get on the tale of Billy the Kid in court, which may or may not have happened, but which is a good story regardless.

Billy, so the story goes, had just been found guilty by a jury in Lincoln. He was now about to be sentenced by this representative of a law that he had little regard for. The judge looked solemnly over his desk at Billy the Kid, made his little set speech and ended in tones of deep portent: ''I thereby sentence you to be hanged by the neck until you are dead—dead—dead!''

"Old bozo," said Billy, or such words as passed for the same in those parlous days. "Old bozo, you're full of the well known bunk. Before they ever hang *me* in Lincoln county, the top of your crown will be red—red—red.'' He emphasized the words by leaning far over and pointing deliberately at the judge's thatch.

The judge was white-headed and the chances of his ever reaching the state prophesied by Billy the Kid were extremely remote. The chances of hanging Billy the Kid were also just as remote, though no one seeing him then with guns covering him and manacles restraining him would ever have believed it.

"For such words as those, young man," said the judge, "you could get a mighty stiff sentence for contempt of court. You *would* get it if it weren't for the fact that you are to be hanged instead."

Billy answered him just as amiably.

"Don't go breathing hard, old monkey face," he said politely, "with the thought that anybody's ever going to hang *me*. That goes for your Lincoln county or any other. Don't go gettin' no remorse about sentencin' *me* to be hung. *Adios*, old fish face!''

And Billy walked jauntily from the presence of his majesty. As he went prancing along with his usual air of bravado, he turned to the sheriff, who accompanied him.

"Pat, to make that hanging a success I'll have to be there, won't I?"

"I reckon you will, Billy," answered Mr. Garret.

"Well," said the Kid, "I allow as how you'll have to put 'er off, Pat. I'm simply not agoin' to be on hand that morning."

Which was as true a word as ever uttered by mortal man. The Kid took advantage of a hand that was smaller than his wrist to free his hands from the bands of steel put there by the weight of the law. He did this two days before he was due to depart this earth by order of the court. He proceeded forthwith to kill the two men who had steadily kept guard over him, and he terrorized the town of Lincoln while attending to the little preliminaries of having a blacksmith batter off his leg chains and manacles and while he requisitioned a horse from a man who cared very little about giving it up.

He left Lincoln in a very cheerful frame of mind. As he reached a juncture in the trail where a point of rock were going to hide him from further view, he turned, waved his sombrero at the crowd, and yelled:

"Three cheers for Billy the Kid!"

It is not too much to suspect that Mr. Bonney was well pleased with his endeavors.

CHAPTER EIGHT

ELFEGO AS SHERIFF

Mr. Elfego Baca was elected sheriff of Socorro County, a man-sized job in a tough principality as large as many a hectic European state. The details of the contest are now hazy. Whether he was elected because it was his turn at the political pump, or because of the fond remembrance of Robin Hood at the Kelly store of Shaw and Baca, or because of the fracas at Frisco, is not now of considerable importance. Elfego was sheriff, fittingly ensconced in the same court house where he had once been tried for his life, and boss of the jail where he had spent such langourous hours after the Frisco trouble.

It was a sensation to be remembered, and Mr. Baca put his feet upon the desk of the sheriff of Socorro County, and accepted the homage of his henchmen. Surrounded by his trusty deputies, Elfego prepared to make old Socorro safe for all worthy humans.

In due course the grand jury met, handed down indictments, and started the active business of sheriff Baca's office. Mr. Baca was cool in the midst of his excited deputies. Warrants were made out and the deputies strained at the leash awaiting the orders of the big boss.

"Calm yourselves," said Mr. Baca, "and send in the chief clerk."

The chief clerk entered.

"Take that list of the people wanted and send this letter to them," said Mr. Baca, sitting back in his swivel chair and preparing for words.

"Dear sir," dictated Elfego to the chief clerk. "I have a warrant here for your arrest. Please come in by March 15 and give yourself up. If you don't I'll know that you intend to resist arrest, and I will feel justified in shooting you on sight when I come after you. Yours truly, Elfego Baca, sheriff."

It was one of the most efficient methods of sheriffing ever adopted on the American continent. The gentlemen whose names were on warrants would come into the office of the sheriff, lay their gats carefully on the table, and say cheerily: "Hello, Mr. Baca. I'm here."

It was really an occasion of great social significance. There were smiles on both sides, appropriate words were spoken, and the needed gentlemen were led away to inspect their future apartments in the county jail. Nothing could be simpler, nothing could be more efficient, nothing could be so neat.

There was one retort that came in answer to Mr. Baca's epistle. It was in the form of a return epistle, which read:

"Ef yu want me, you blankety blank Mexican, cum and git me. i will be under the big cottonwood by the river at noon wednesday.

ART FORD."

"*Madre de Dios!*" breathed the deputies.
"Certainly, you are—"

"Sure, I'm going," said Elfego. "Ain't I
been invited?"

"But, Elfego—"

"You stay here or I'll make a mistake and
shoot you. Mr. Ford asks me to come. He didn't
ask you."

And next day at noon, Elfego walked up to
the big cottonwood by the river and waited in vain
for the appearance of the belligerent and ungram-
matical Mr. Ford. He returned to his office to
find Mr. Ford—already disarmed and entirely
amiable—waiting there for him. There were no
recriminations. It had simply been a case of over-
exuberant penmanship on the part of Mr. Ford
and no harm was done. Mr. Ford was assigned to
his future lodgings, smiles were exchanged, and
an unhappy incident was closed with best wishes
on all sides.

Mr. Baca could rest a bit on the reputation he
had made in previous years as deputy sheriff—a
reputation of significance in the great and turbu-
lent state of New Mexico.

Notorious among all cases was that of Jose
Garcia, who had killed a man in Belen and carried

off the man's wife as prize. Garcia had escaped very neatly and had been forgotten. The lady had not been loathe to accompany Garcia, being in few words, the sweet instigator of the murder. Their retreat into the mountains was a complete success.

The next sight of the lady in question was not a pretty one. Sheepherders had come across the form of a human being cut into four parts and strung up on the limb of a tree much as is done with a butchered animal. From evidence accumulating it was soon proved that the body was that of Garcia's late inamorata. Garcia was absent again, as usual, with a two day start on a good horse. The chances didn't look promising for the deputy sheriff. It was not a question of dashing off in search of a fresh trail, but in going to work very laboriously to follow up the cold tracks of the murderer.

As a matter of fact it was a tedious job of three months in the style of Sherlock Holmes and not at all in the manner of a spectacular western sheriff. The trail of Garcia was faint, and led to the wilds of Sandoval County where he was said to be herding sheep with an outfit noted for its disregard both for the law and the niceties of polite society. It was on outfit that took unkindly to the approach of any stranger, no matter how well intentioned. It contained in its ranks gentlemen who could have little or no comfort in a court of law, and were rather set against being honored in such manner.

The pursuit was a matter that required ingenuity coupled with considerable fortitude. Elfego proceeded to Bernalillo, county seat of Sandoval, and enlisted the services of young Afredo Montoya, then a boy of sixteen but later a very successful sheriff of the county. Young Montoya was not acquainted with Garcia and only faintly aware of the nature of the quest. He had been selected as Elfego Baca's guide because he was contitutionally of such curious bent as to have traversed every foot of Sandoval County in times past. In Bernalillo it was quite generally conceded that if anybody knew anything about Sandoval County it was young Alfredo.

The young gentleman guide first became aware of the nature of his undertaking when, on getting a dozen miles distant from the town's confines, Elfego stopped to complete his disguise. With burnt cork, the undersheriff of Socorro County painstakingly blackened up his face with the aid of a tiny pocket mirror until he looked like a cross between Al Jolson and Lew Dockstader. There was the difference that while Al and the late Lew could get by with black gloves of funeral hue, Mr. Baca was under the necessity of blackening every part of his well set anatomy that might be subject to the scrutiny of the public. It was the work of one solid half day, counting times out for the preparing of more minstrel cork and the violent damning of match burns. From it young Montoya gained valuable make-up experience that was to be utterly wasted on his native land. Elfego reached what he could with the burnt cork, and had to trust to the integrity of Alfredo in covering the more inaccessible portions of his frame. Should the black face of Jolson fail in a critical moment it would only be the signal for Broadway convulsions. Should the black face of Mr. Elfego Baca fail in like circumstances it would mean the music of heavenly angels. That was the great difference between blacking up in the mountains of Sandoval county and in the dressing room of a New York playhouse. Rather a nice distinction of difference—to come right down to it.

The parade began with Alfredo in the lead and his colored servant, Elfego, following along behind. It took six long days to come upon the location of the camp which supposedly housed the dangerous Garcia. Six long days and six long nights when Elfego thought it best not to sleep too soundly for fear of what the darkness might hold. There was the chance that friends of Garcia in Bernalillo were already in advance of the Elfego Baca party carrying the news to the sheep camp. In that event the disguise of Elfego would mean nothing but that an unknown gentleman of dusky hue would find a grave in Sandoval county and there would be the mystery of the sudden and com-

plete disappearance of a deputy sheriff of Socorro
County to account for.

There were times when young Montoya was
not so sure of his sense of direction. The sheep
outfit was supposed to be where Alfredo and Elfego discovered it not to be. There was cogitation
over this and just a slight touch of apprehension
having to do with thoughts of ambush. The decision to go on was made as much from the feeling
that it was as safe to go on as to go back.

It was on the evening of the sixth day that
Alfredo and Elfego saw the fires of the sheep outfit. The sun was going down and there were
mysterious shadows creeping about the sagebrush.
The sheepherders were preparing supper, and
Alfredo and Elfego paused to reconnoitre. The
question now was whether Alfredo should go in
alone and look the situation over, or whether it
would be safer and more effective for Elfego—
blackfaced within an inch of his life—to accompany him. Elfego was eager for action. Garcia
was somewhere right ahead. It was a matter now
of Garcia or Baca, and it might as well be decided
at once as later on. It would be little good for
Alfredo to go in alone anyhow, because he didn't
know Garcia and it was not a time for cross examination.

Young Alfredo and his colored groom Elfego
proceeded, therefore, to ride up over the edge of
a small arroyo and into the sheepherders' camp.

The sheep outfit was of such magnitude that the old time shepherd with his crook would have been lost in the shuffle. The men were mounted and the horses stood munching lazily near the supper fire. The baaing of the lambs settling down for the night was accompaniment for Alfredo and his dusky friend. They came slowly through the rapidly falling dusk, and the sheep outfit arose with suspicion to greet them.

"Ay!" shouted Alfredo cheerily, "it's me!"

And there was a general dropping of hands from holsters, and relaxation all along the line.

"Alfredo!" they shouted in return. "It's Alfredo!" they shouted to one another in relief. "Come in, Alfredo. You're just in time for supper."

"My groom," said Alfredo, waving a hasty hand in the direction of Elfego, whose presence— duly noted—had caused a second sudden tightening of sheepherders' faces, and pistol fingers. They examined closely, and turned about with smiles.

"*Negros*," they said, with chuckles, and pointed to Elfego and laughed with one another.

They were eased, and Elfego was eased for a minute, but his eyes were working furiously to find Garcia. He found him in the background, standing by his horse, and keeping his gaze on the scene while his fingers were working industriously with a lariat that hung from the saddle. There

was also hanging from the saddle, Elfego dis
cerned at once, a holster containing a gun. It was
noticeable that Garcia's fingers at work on the
lariat were within six inches of the holster.

Garcia was watching the colored groom with
hawk-like glance. Elfego had dismounted hastily
and was now holding the stirrup of Alfredo while
he got off his horse. No groom at an ancient Brit-
ish inn could have done it with more adeptness
and true servility. Elfego was careful that his
face should be in the direction of Garcia while he
carried out his groom-like chores.

Garcia for the first time seemed convinced.
He relaxed for an instant to throw the lariat over
the saddle horn. For a second his face was turned
from Elfego. When it turned back, Garcia was
faced by two Colt pistols with openings the size
of miniature cannons, and he knew that the game
was over.

"Up" said the harsh voice of Elfego. "Throw
'em up, and move away from that horse! Pronto,
now! Yup! Yup!"

That voice could belong to only one man in
the world.

"Elfego Baca," breathed Garcia, and moved.

Alfredo in the meantime was covering the
three others grouped about the fire.

"Up!" said Alfredo in good imitation of
Elfego, and three pairs of sheepherder's hands
went aloft.

"Around toward the fire!" ordered Elfego, and Garcia found himself grouped with his companions.

"Get all the guns, Alfredo," said Elfego, relieving young Montoya of his shooting responsibility.

Alfredo went over them carefully under the direction of Elfego, relieving the gentlemen of the guns on their persons and carefully examining saddle bags and other likely hiding places. He then took his lariat and pinned the arms of Garcia.

Elfego made the others a little speech.

"This man Garcia," he said pointing, "is a murderer. He killed his wife and cut her in four pieces . . . . in four pieces. A very bad man. We are taking him back to Socorro. Alfredo will ride on ahead to show the way. Garcia will come next and then me. You will stay here. You know Alfredo's father. He knows you, and he knows that Alfredo is up here to visit you. If Alfredo doesn't come back or if anything happens to Alfredo, Alfredo's father will come up here and kill you. Remember that, and don't try to move from this camp after we leave!"

Garcia was put on his horse. Elfego's lariat was placed about the waist of Garcia and the other end tied securely to the saddle horn of Elfego. Alfredo rode on ahead to show the way, Garcia came next on his horse, and Elfego made the third in the procession. Alfredo took a short cut; there

was no annoyance from the three cowed sheepherders, and while it had taken six days to get to
where the sheep outfit was, it took only eight hours
to return to the little town of Thornton on the railroad.

The appearance of the strange trio in Thornton—now Domingo—was occasion for a demon-
stration that augured poorly for the earthly con-
tinuance of Mr. Garcia. When once it was clear
who the gentleman in ropes was, there was a decided inclination to relieve Mr. Baca of his responsibility. The three hastily retreated to the
little red Santa Fe railroad station with the mob
in pursuit. Elfego relieved Garcia of his thongs
and prepared to protect his life. Alfredo looked
askance at unfettering the murderer.

"Never mind," said Elfego looking through
the window of the station at the crowd without.
"Garcia isn't going to make a break. Look out
there!"

It wasn't necessary for Garcia to look out
there. He realized without being told that the last
place he wanted to be was outside the protection
of one Elfego Baca. There was absolutely no
danger of Elfego losing him in the circumstances.

"When's the next train for Albuquerque?"
said Elfego to the station agent, waving a careless
gun.

"Four hours," answered that worthy.

"*Madre de Dios!*" muttered Garcia, edging

around behind the stove away from the door of
the depot.

"When's the next train anywhere?" demanded Elfego.

"Fifteen minutes—going the other way,"
said the agent.

The crowd was pressing around the door,
awaiting courage to come in and claim Garcia.
There was loud talk, agitated shouts from those
in the rear.

"What do you want?" asked Elfego—aca-
demically, be it admitted, for he was well aware
of the nature of their desires. There was also a
certain measure of irritability about Mr. Baca
having to do with the nature of his quest for
Garcia. This Sherlock Holmes business wasn't to
his liking, and he was more than a little sorry that
he hadn't captured Garcia in a free-for-all, bang-
bang battle.

"We want Garcia," said the mob, realizing
not at all the thoughts racing through the head of
Mr. Baca, and being—at the same time—quite unaware of the reputation of the gentleman they
were addressing. "We want Garcia. Murderer.
Asesino!" The last was a shout.

"Keep back!" said Elfego sharply to the unfortunate ones who were in the front row and who
were being pushed—much against their volition—
dangerously close to the fearful vision that con-
fronted them.

Those in the front rank were not bitten by a desire to proceed any further. In addition to the two wicked looking gats handled carelessly by Mr. Baca, they were faced by the fearful visage of the deputy sheriff of Socorro county, who resembled nothing so much as a native African who had been frightened half white by occurrences of more than ordinary importance. The black cork had worn off in spots, leaving behind a spooky, breath-taking, unearthly countenance warranted to make pause the most intrepid mob member.

"Give us Garcia!" howled the mob members from the rear. "*Asesino!*" "Murderer!"

This, be it understood, was clamor almost entirely from mob members farthest from the door. Those near the door were faced by the enigmatic and tight-lipped and eminently dangerous smile of Elfego Baca. There was within them the desire to knock Elfego away from there and get to Garcia, but they were combated by a steady, steely eye which was reinforced by two malevolent looking Colt pistols.

"*Asesino!* Bring him out! Lynch him!"

Elfego, disdainful of the crowd he was dealing with and reckless anyhow at the thought of having these people interfering in a matter that didn't concern them, bided his time. He sensed that there would be a moment for his words.

"*Asesino!*" howled the mob on the outskirts.

"Go on in! Bring him out! Knock that hombre down at the door! Go on! Go ON!"

Elfego stood waiting, with his legs well apart and his guns braced against his thighs. He spoke now, very deliberately.

"Keep back!" he said in a biting, soothing, insinuating voice, that bore an aroma of subtle poison to those nearest at hand. "Keep back, if you want to stay alive!"

Unconsciously those in the front rank fell back. They were met by the maddened howls of those pushing from the rear.

"What the hell! Go on! GO ON! Who're you afraid of! Get that hombre out of there!"

"Keep back!" said Elfego, seemingly the least worried man on the premises.

"You'd better get out of the road, and let us take that prisoner of yours in peace," said a more sensible member of the mob. "You'll get hurt. We're going to string up that fellow."

"You might get him," said Elfego slowly. "But you'll have to take me with him. He's my prisoner and you can't have him."

"You'll get hurt," said the mob member.

"Maybe," said Elfego, "but I have two guns here and twelve shots. The first move from you birds means at least four of you pumped full of lead."

"Who the hell are you?" demanded a voice from the crowd.

For some reason there was interest in the answer. Silence fell over that part of the crowd that could best see Mr. Baca. There seemed a genuine curiosity as to his identity.

"I" said Elfego, in the silence. "I am Elfego Baca."

A knowing murmur of wonderment and awed recognition swept over the crowd, closely followed by the shrill whistle of the approaching train. Elfego knew it as the proper moment for speech.

"I'm going to put Garcia on this train," he informed the mob tensely. "And anybody who tries to stop me or who tries to get close to Garcia has me to kill . . . . Does anybody wish to annoy Senor Garcia?"

He drew out the words softly, insinuatingly, and pointed them with a look of the eye and a motion of his gun fingers. The train had pulled in and ground to a stop.

"Get back!" commanded Elfego, waving a path in front of the door. "Get back, and quick about it!"

The crowd fell back and the shouts in the background died away as knowledge of whom they were dealing with filtered out to the obstreperous ones in the distance. Afredo went out first, carefully holding his two guns in battle formation. A highly uncomfortable, but withal brave, Garcia, walked steadily after him, and faced the crowd without flinching. Elfego brought up the rear,

covering as many of the leading members of the
mob as possible, and wheeling at the steps of the
smoking car to cover the entire gathering. Garcia
and Alfredo hurriedly mounted the steps and disappeared within. Elfego stood at the foot of the
steps and faced the mob until the brakeman gave
the signal and the train began to move slowly
away from the town of Thornton.

Elfego still covered the crowd from the top
of the smoking car steps, half hoping that there
would be need of marksmanship. He wheeled
hastily at a shout that swept up from below. He
prepared for the worst. The shout was:

"Adios, Elfego; good luck!"

And Elfego had scarcely time to change his
countenance into a surprised smile before the
train swept by the water tank which passed in
Thornton as the city limits.

CHAPTER NINE

SHERIFF BACA CUTS DOWN THE JAIL FOOD BILL

On one of their periodic forays on the territorial legislature, the sheep men had pushed through a bill that practically made debt a jail offense. The sheep industry is highly seasonable and as a consequence the sheepmen were required to tide their employes over the off seasons. If a man contracted a debt to the sheep owners at that time and failed for any reason to pay it out in work when work was available, he was liable for a period of sixty days in jail. In the face of it the bill looked honest enough, but it has since been discarded as fostering a very definite form of peonage.

While still sheriff of Socorro County, Elfego Baca returned from a trip to Albuquerque to find his jail cluttered up with eleven prisoners all starting to serve sixty-day sentences under the new law. One man with a wife and four children dependent on him was doing his sixty-day stint, Elfego found, because of failure to pay a debt of $11. Questioning of the others brought out similar tales that added to the aroma of putridity that hung about the whole procedure.

After slight cogitation, Sheriff Elfego Baca called the eleven culprits into his office and conferred with them. Aside from the question of justice was the thought of Socorro County being burdened with the care of feeding eleven prisoners for sixty days just for the pleasure of making a few prominent sheepmen feel good. It was fairly obvious that the unfortunate gentlemen would be of little service in meeting their indebtedness while resting in the *carcel* at Socorro. After which thought, Mr. Sheriff Baca released the eleven prisoners and sent them back to their homes.

"Get out," said the sheriff with bluff kindness. "Go on back home and go to work. Pay off your debts. You'll only eat us poor here."

So one week after their sixty days' sentence had begun, the eleven were as free again as the scurrying clouds above.

The news was not slow in getting around and Elfego was summoned to the telephone that night. It was a call from Los Lunas. The speaker was Harry Owens, district attorney.

"Hello, Elfego, is that you?"

"Yes."

"How are things getting along down there?"

"Fine,"—heartily. "Just fine!"

"Everything all right at the jail?"

"Yep, the jail's fine—just fine . . . . . . Everything fine at the jail."

"Um-uh . . . . Having good weather, I suppose?"

"Fine weather," said Mr. Baca, enthusiastically, knowing perfectly well where Mr. Owens was headed for.

"Any trouble with the prisoners at the jail?"

"Not a bit," said Elfego. "Everything fine at the jail."

"Prisoners all well, eh?"

"Fine," said Elfego. "Just fine."

"How many prisoners you got there now?"

"None," said Elfego.

"None, ... Well, uh . . . . Well, now . . . . None!"

"None," said Elfego. "They ate too much."

"Well, did anybody tell you? . . . . You know, of course . . . . "

"They're gone," said Elfego. "I chased them out. They ate too much."

"Well, you know, now . . . . the court . . . . "

"They're gone," said Elfego, "and they're not coming back. I won't let 'em in."

"Well, Mr. Baca, you know . . . . Legally . . . . Very serious."

"Sure," said Elfego. "I know. But they're gone. They ate too much."

Which was as far as the district attorney ever got, and which was in effect the end of the debt contract law. Not that other sheriffs went to the lengths of Elfego Baca, but that district judges suddenly decided it was a poor law and acted accordingly. The legislature repealed it before the supreme court had a chance to rule it out.

Modern methods of prison management as first exemplified by Warden Osborne at Sing Sing and later carried forward by other wardens of humanitarian principles were in part antici- pated by Sheriff Elfego Baca.

There was the case of two cowboys of a rough nature who resided in the same cell and took out their exercise in cursing the guards and stirring up the other prisoners to mutiny. One, with guile comparable to the well known fox, prevailed upon the jailer to promote him to the position of cook upon the release of the gentleman who had hither- to held down the honor. Said prevailing was done during the absence of Sheriff Baca, who, upon his return, found that the psuedo cook had taken French leave of the jail following a particularly terrible supper prepared by his far from expert hands.

This had been the only prisoner to make his getaway during the regime of Sheriff Baca and the matter called for deep meditation. From that meditation emerged a full blown idea, and Elfego called for the other bard-boiled buzzard who had been the cell mate of the quondam cook.

"I want your help, Fisher," said Sheriff Baca when the jailer brought in the prisoner.

"Me, Mr. Baca?" said Fisher. "How can I help you?"

"You can tell me where Watson is," said Elfego.

"Me!" said Fisher with astonishment. "How should I know where he is?"

"Well, you ought to," said Elfego. " You helped him frame the getaway."

Fisher looked at him from under dark brows, and suddenly flared up.

"Sure, I helped him, the dirty blankety blank," he said tensely, "and then he goes off and forgets me."

Elfego smiled and patted him on the shoulder.

"Forget it," he said kindly. "Come on out and have supper with me."

And they went down to the Chinaman's where Mr. Baca plied Fisher with potatoes and vegetables and a T-bone steak as big as the largest plate in the establishment and almost as thick.

"Why don't you go out and bring that dirty bum back?" ventured Elfego at the height of the feast.

"Me?" said Fisher, managing to squeeze that much through teeth that were acting as sideboards to protect the mass within his face.

"Sure, you," said Mr. Baca. "He'll think you got out yourself. You can walk right up to him and tell him how you did it. I'll give you a deputy sheriff badge, and the jailer's gun, and these handcuffs . . . . . and seventy-five dollars in cash. If you bring that guy back, I'll see that you don't have much trouble getting off light with the judge. How does that strike you?"

Mr. Fisher was too polite to say that it struck him the sheriff had gone loose from his moorings, but the violent effect he made to swallow all he had eaten in one gulp testified to his feelings.

"You don't seem to be worryin' about *me* comin' back," he said finally.

"Oh, you'll come back all right," said Mr. Baca, "or I'll come after you and bring you back."

The affair was settled and Fisher started. It was only after he was gone that Sheriff Baca began to have serious thoughts about his plan. He felt it incumbent upon himself to bring the tidings to Judge Mechem, who was then District Judge and later was to be Governor of New Mexico.

"You gave the fellow seventy-five dollars, and a gun, and a badge and your handcuffs!" said the astonished judge.

"Sure, I did," admitted Elfego proudly. "He'll come back all right. If he doesn't, I'm ready to resign."

"If he doesn't, you won't need to resign," said the judge significantly.

"It's going to work out all right," said Elfego.

"It's worked out fine already for Fisher," said the cynical judge. "He has your seventy-five and a gun, and you have just one less prisoner."

As the week dragged on, Elfego began to have qualms about the propriety of trusting bad boys of the type of Fisher. He had visions of Fisher

**Elfego (on the left) and a few of the boys at Roswell, start-
ing out for an afternoon of pleasure.**

communing in high glee with Watson. He had visions of Fisher toasting Watson with foaming brew bought with the seventy-five dollars of Sheriff Elfego Baca. There were very bad visions, and they were not bettered by the remarks that began to float about the court house at Socorro.

"Heard anything from Fisher?" was the morning greeting of Sheriff Baca.

"Didn't expect to," replied Sheriff Baca. "Sent him out to do a job; didn't expect him to be writing me a book."

"Haven't heard anything from Fisher, eh," said the solicitous voices next morning. "Ought to be hearing something soon—if you're going to hear at all, don't you think?"

"Nope," said Sheriff Baca, keeping his goat tightly in rein, and assuming a fine nonchalance that he was beginning not to feel.

It may as well be admitted that it was a long week in the life of Elfego Baca. It was broken by a telegram that reached Sheriff Baca in Santa Fe, where he had fled to get away from his kindly Socorro friends. It was a telegram from Mr. Fisher. Before Mr. Baca could have the privilege of perusing the elongated message, he was forced to part with the enormous sum of $8.75. Mr. Baca had only been partly right about Mr. Fisher writing the book. He had refrained while on the hunt, but when once his quarry had been captured, he felt the call of authorship upon him.

Mr. Fisher reported that he had captured Mr. Watson. He reported in considerable detail that he had captured Mr. Watson. In telegraphic words of great value, he reported exactly how Mr. Watson had looked when first he gazed at his old friend, Mr. Fisher. He reported—despite the exorbitant Western Union rates—exactly where Mr. Watson had stood, what Mr. Watson had said, what Mr. Fisher had said in return, what might have happened if Mr. Watson had done one thing and Mr. Fisher had not done another, what did happen, how proud Mr. Fisher was of what had happened, how nonplussed Mr. Watson was by the same set of circumstances. It omitted no detail of the great bravery of one Joseph Fisher, but lately of the county jail of Socorro. It was a full $8.75 worth. It finished with the classic words:

"What shall I do with him?"

Upon receiving which—report hath it—Sheriff Baca placed his hand to his overheated brow, and was only kept from a fell swoon by the weight of the pressing responsibility that now devolved upon him.

"My God," said Sheriff Baca in a muted breath. "What shall he do with him!"

Whereupon the exasperated, and greatly re lieved and a bit bewildered Sheriff Baca sat himself down according to report and indited the following:

"Kiss him twice and bring him in you damn
fool."

Exactly ten words, and ten very good words,
it must be admitted.

Among those brought within the toils of the
law by the mail order business of Sheriff Baca
was the famous Henry Coleman, one of the very
last of the bad men of New Mexico. Coleman was
reputed to be the black sheep of a good Texas
family, one member of which was for long years
Congressman from that state. Coleman was,
necessarily, not his real name.

Coleman did a fine business west of Socorro
in appropriating the cattle of his neighbors and
shooting such remonstrants as arose from that
connection. There was once a young and ambitious
lawyer from Gallup who proceeded to Socorro to
serve a writ of attachment against some cattle
that Henry Coleman had bought from a friend and
failed to make remittance for. The young attorney
was one Arthur T. Hannett, who was later to be
Governor of New Mexico.

Young Mr. Hannett was totally unaware of
the character of the gentleman he had come to
deal with. In the exuberance of youth and because his law practice had not yet attained the
magnitude that would allow him to ignore such a
troublesome matter as serving a writ of attachment, Mr. Hannett was extremely anxious to get
in touch with Mr. Henry Coleman. In his anxiety

he attempted to enlist the services of various and sundry deputy sheriffs and constables and peace officers.

"I have a writ of attachment I want served," young Hannett would say to the officer accosted.

"A writ—sure!" would say the officer, heartily. "Who on?"

"Henry Coleman," Hannett would answer, hurrying the last syllable for the sake of his listener who was rapidly backing away.

"Henry Coleman?" the officer would repeat, as if striving mightily to bring a picture of the man to mind. "Henry Coleman? I do not know heem . . . . " A sorrowful shrug of the shoulders.

"Well, he runs a big cattle ranch out here," Hannett would persist. "Surely you know him."

"Eh, well . . . . Maybe . . . . Eh, yes, Henry Coleman . . . . But I do not know where at ees heem . . . . "

And young Hannett would suddenly find himself alone in the dusty road which ran through Socorro. It was a bewildering business. Before the end of the first day of attempts to get in touch with Henry Coleman, Mr. Hannett was struck by the fact that he was being strictly avoided by gentlemen wearing official badges. So far as young Hannett could discover, Socorro was absolutely at the mercy of a criminal horde. It was quite evident that the legal forces of the town and county had departed for unknown regions.

Greatly mystified and considerably worried, Hannett went to call on a fellow attorney in the city. After explanation he asked the lawyer gentleman the cause of the leprosy taint that seemed to surround him.

"You've come down to Socorro," said the lawyer slowly, "you've come down to Socorro to serve a writ on Henry Coleman!" The friendly lawyer seemed to wish to disregard the plain evidence of which his ears were cognizant.

"Yes, sir," said young Hannett staunchly, "on Henry Coleman."

"On Henry Coleman!" said the lawyer, evidently still reluctant to believe that his hearing was competent.

"Yes, sir," said young Hannett, innocently and bravely.

There was a lengthy pause.

"My boy," said the lawyer finally, putting a kindly hand on Hannett's shoulder. "You wouldn't think of going down to Washington to serve a writ on the President, would you?"

"No-o," said Hannett dubiously.

"You wouldn't think of descending on London to serve a writ on King George, would you?" continued the lawyer.

"No-o," said young Hannett unsteadily.

"You wouldn't think of trying to serve a writ

of attachment on a runaway locomotive, would you?" pursued the lawyer.

Young Mr. Hannett admitted that there might be some difficulty in pursuing his duties in that special regard.

"Well, then," said the lawyer kindly, "you go right on back to Gallup and forget about those cows. You couldn't get the entire national guard in this part of the country to attempt to serve a writ of attachment or anything else on Henry Coleman. Henry Coleman is simply not the kind of man people serve writs on."

So young Arthur Hannett, who was later to become Governor of the great state of New Mexico, wended his way back to Gallup with the conviction that while the law might be distinctly remunerative in some of its branches, litigation concerning Henry Coleman was not one of them. He decided to let Henry Coleman stew in his own juice. Which was just as well for Arthur Hannett, for Henry Coleman was a man who handled a gun as carelessly as the ordinary human being handles an umbrella.

Coleman did come in and give up on the written request of Sheriff Baca, but he was able to convince a jury that he did nothing out of the way in dispatching the few souls who deigned to enter into slight disagreements with himself. He convinced a Socorro county jury satisfactorily enough, but he failed to carry out his responsibilities to himself in drawing with sufficient alacrity in an altercation in a saloon shortly afterward and a slow, solemn procession eventually escorted him off to his final resting place. It was conceded to be a fitting solution to a bad situation, and his assailant had little to be fearful of with the exception of a possible laurel wreath from a grateful public.

CHAPTER TEN

Elfego Discovers That the Mexican Revolution is a Free-for-all Fight. He Enters

The Madero revolution broke out in Mexico in 1910; old Porfirio Diaz was dethroned, and a mad scramble was on. It was an open, free-for-all fight and there was no doubt but that Elfego Baca would be in it sooner or later. He came in officially as the American representative of Huerta. But before that he mixed with all the great figures of Mexico's turmoil—Madero, Carranza, Villa, Huerta, Orozco, Salazar, and half a hundred others.

Madero, to start with, was of a family of wealthy distillers, making mescal, tequila, sotol, and conaque (cognac). In addition to that, rumor hath it, he was a spiritualist, and was early visited with a vision that proclaimed him the future ruler of Mexico. Along this line, he wrote a book castigating the regime of Diaz and advocating a house cleaning. He was promptly arrested by Diaz and confined. Diaz, still at the summit of his power, so far allowed his rage to get the better of him as to arrest Madero's wife and throw her into jail as well. It was poor judgment. Madero's going to the lockup would have meant little in the life of Mexico City where Old

General Fierro (1), the only man unafraid of Pancho Villa, and Villa (2), who finally killed Fierro in cold blood while he was struggling to ford a mountain stream in Chihuahua.

Porfirio got his fun from bouncing obstreperous complainers, but it happened that Madero's wife was of very good family, and was young, and was beautiful. The sympathy of the people was immediately on the side of the Maderos.

It was at this time that Orozco—a name later to be reckoned with in Mexican politics—came into the picture. Orozco was a freighter at the Green mine, which was owned by American capital and of which Albert B. Fall was attorney. Orozco's mother had read Madero's book and was also properly shocked by the incarceration of Senora Madero. She said in part to her son: "Pascual, you either follow Madero and do what you can to make his ideas come true or you're no son of mine."

Orozco bent his efforts to pleasing his mother. At the start he had his own six shooter and recruited six additional rifles of such ancient vintage that it was difficult to secure ammunition for them. Secret organizations were formed, secret meetings were held, vows were made, and things began to take a bad turn for Old Porfirio Diaz. There were rumblings of mutiny in his army, and plain evidences of treachery. The story of how Porfirio finally departed for Europe, leaving behind him an epistle which deplored conditions in his country and said that he was willing to decamp rather than have bloodshed on his behalf, is part of history. It meant that Madero was boss. He became provisional president, and had as his supporters all the firebrands who were to cause his death later.

But what interests us now is the part of Elfego Baca in it all. His introduction to the leading characters came in 1906, when he met Pancho Villa, known then as Pancho Jaime, in the mining town of Parral. Villa was already a bandit with a bounty over his head of twelve years standing. He came in to sell Baca mules that he had recently removed from under the control of their proper owners. Baca was in Parral not so much for mining as for a look at Gillette, the American cattle thief for whose capture a reward of $50,000 had been offered in Kansas City.

Elfego had been on the trail for Gillette for months. He had missed him in New Mexico when Gillette had left a snow bound train and taken a different route to Old Mexico. Elfego had by chance written to his friend, Charley Hunt, who ran a saloon in Parral, telling him of Gillette and asking him to be on the lookout for him. The letter reached Parral before Gillette did. When Gillette arrived, Hunt was ready for him. In the pleasant way of Mexico, Gillette and Hunt immediately formed a compact by which Gillette would give Hunt the $50,000 in lieu of reward and Hunt would return to Kansas City to report the death of Gillette and settle up such minor affairs

as Gillette—the "Million Dollar Cattle Thief"—
had left on his sudden departure.

When Elfego reached Parral things were in
that status. He had first to learn from Kansas
City whether the $50,000 reward still remained
good before taking proper action. His plan was
to kidnap Gillette and get him back on American
soil before making the arrest. Villa could come in
handy for that purpose and Elfego talked to him
along that line. Would Pancho Jaime undertake
to get Gillette to the American border for the sum
of one thousand dollars? Answered Pancho
Jaime decidedly: "I will take Gillette and his
wife and his horse and buggy *all* to the American
line for one thousand dollars."

A very efficient man—Pancho Jaime, later to
be Pancho Villa—but there was no necessity for
his good offices after all. Word came from Kansas City that the reward was no longer standing.

The next sight of Villa and the first sight of
Orozco was across from the smelter at El Paso a
few days before the battle of Juarez in 1911. The
Federalists held the town. The Madero forces
surrounded it. And Elfego Baca heard stories of
a man named Pancho Villa, who had formerly
been a bandit and had 500 men as wild as himself
and who was now part of the Orozco forces.

Elfego wanted to see this Pancho. He had a
suspicion who he might be. He went across the
border and sought out Orozco. Could by any

chance this Pancho Villa be the Pancho Jaime of Parral? He described the Pancho Jaime of Parral, and Orozco allowed as how there was a great possibility of Pancho being Pancho. Pancho was over the hills about two miles resting with his bad boys, but he would be here for a meeting about eleven o'clock, if Elfego cared to wait.

Elfego was there at eleven o'clock, as was Madero and others of his staff. Madero had the pleasure of reading to Villa his new commission as colonel and Elfego had the pleasure of greeting his old friend and explaining to him what the commission was all about. Villa had got to the point of laboriously getting on paper in a scrawly hand the words: "Francisco Villa," but there his literary inspiration had ceased for life.

"This paper," explained Elfego patiently, "is your appointment as colonel."

"What the hell," said Villa. "Fight! That's me. That dam paper . . . . What do I care?"

Anyhow, Pancho was colonel, Orozco was general, and Madero—with his side kick, Carranza—was there to represent the government as commander-and-chief. Madero was really of too fine strain to be mixed up with his own forces. For one thing, he objected to the attack of Juarez because of the bloodshed that would follow and the innocent citizens who would suffer. That, to Villa and Orozco, was so much apple sauce.

Orozco and Villa met in El Paso to discuss the

outrage. They were further incensed by the publication of a hand bill by one Tamborin, supporter of the faction retaining Juarez, to the effect that Orozco and Villa were bandits and outlaws who lacked the courage to attack the town. With Villa was an aide-de-camp wearing a blue shirt; with Orozco was an aide-de-camp wearing a red shirt. The plan, as hatched by Orozco and Villa in an El Paso barber shop, was for blue shirt and red shirt to make their way down the Mexican side of the Rio Grande to the International bridge and open fire on the Federalist outposts stationed there.

So ordered, so done. Red shirt and blue shirt, who were aide-de-camps only by title and rough cookies by nature, made their way down to the bridge and opened fire. The fire was returned briskly. It was the signal for Orozco and Villa to dash wildly across the bridge at the smelter and order the advance on Juarez. Madero came up in time to see the rear end of the Orozco-Villa advance clattering up the road on the way to battle. He sent after them a courier bearing a white flag. On order of Orozco, his troops turned just long enough to riddle the unfortunate courier and deposit him in a heap with his flag fluttering about him. The attack got under way.

The battle of Juarez lasted three days and nights, with the defenders having slim chance at any time. The battle cry was: *"Maten pelones!"*

(Shoot anybody with a cap!). The secondary cry was "Shoot Tamborin when there's nobody else to shoot at!" The body of Tamborin, author of the hand bill, lay in the open square, one of the first victims of the raiders. When it attained a final resting place it held the total of 300 bullets—proving anew the rewards of literature.

With victory once won, Madero entered the town as a conquering hero. He came in a high-powered motor car, with flags flying, and bands playing and many bows and much waving of glad hands. With Madero was his wife and his father and his retinue. It was a great occasion—for Madero, but it did nothing but anger Orozco and Villa, the men who had made victory possible and who were now only hangers-on at the grand entrance.

Madero's first official act was also a poor one. He delegated to his father the task of issuing passports to those wishing to enter Juarez. The elder Madero was ensconced in his suite on one of the upper floors of the Hotel Sheldon in El Paso. During the battle all non-combatant natives of Juarez who could get away, got away. They left behind them their cows and chickens and only means of sustenance. To get back it was necessary to have a passport from Papa Madero. To get to Papa Madero it was necessary to enter a swell American hotel and experience the horrors of an American elevator and the none too indulgent favors of haughty American hotel employees.

For the American curiosity hounds who wished to smell the dead bodies stinking in the streets of Juarez it was a simple task to seek out Papa Madero and get their little slip of paper. They came in droves and they cluttered up the streets of Juarez and got in the road of men trying to clear up the debris.

Sheer rage was in the hearts of Orozco and Villa by this time. Orozco issued an order that the Mexican end of the international bridge be closed and nobody be allowed to pass. Papa Madero, himself, with a party of friends, was refused admittance.

"Take," said Papa Madero loftily, "take this note to General Orozco. It will explain who I am."

Orozco, who looked always as much like a general as a scullery maid like a queen, yanked down the tattered garment that passed as a tunic, folded a knee to cover a hole in his trousers, and received the note of Papa Madero. When he realized what it was, he unfolded the knee, spat twice contemptuously on the ground, and addressed the messenger:

"You go back and tell that old fuzzy wuzzy if he puts a step over that bridge, I'll shoot him myself. Tell him if he wants to do anything he can jump in the river. That goes also for his little runt of a son."

Very rough words, and not loyal words

toward the personage of Mr. Madero, now president of the great Republic of Mexico. There were,
to be truthful, bad times in Juarez among the vic-
tors. Bad times ending with a disgraceful scene
in front of the commandant's house before a
crowd of thousands, including many Americans.

Madero was sitting in a chair trying to talk
Orozco out of his grouch. Over in another chair
was the muchly bearded Carranza, whose capacity
with the Madero party was at that time undefined.
Orozco was slouching in another chair, giving no
sign that anything being said by Madero was of
any consequence.

Villa came in, walked up to Madero, took him
firmly by the neck and yanked him clear from his
chair.

"You blankety blank something or other
grandstander," said Villa, dragging the President
of Mexico about roughly by the collar and cursing
him at every step. "If you think we're going to
do all the fighting, and you get all the credit ... "
The gnarled hands of Villa settled about the tender neck of Madero until Madero's eyes began to
pop, and his hands came up in ineffectual attempt
to free the murderous grasp of Villa. It had all
happened in an instant, and without warning.
Villa was backing Madero around the porch before the commandant's house, adding pressure to
his grip at every step and delivering himself of

Mexican curses that had not been heard in Juarez in years.

What Orozco's feelings were it was difficult to tell. His love for Madero was far from intense, but Villa's action warranted discipline. Under officers stood about in a daze. It was Orozco himself who finally freed Madero from Villa's hands. He placed Villa under arrest at once, and had him taken away. For Elfego Baca, who was present, it was also a tense moment. He was the friend of Orozco and he was the friend of Villa. He was afraid of what might happen to Villa, and he didn't care to offend Orozco by saying anything about it.

After he could get back his breath, Madero began making it up with Orozco. He was pleading; he was promising. Orozco was the big man of Mexico; Mexico couldn't get along without him. It was necessary that all friends of Mexico get together now, if anything were ever to be done. Orozco was sullen, but there were pleas from all sides. Finally there was a political handshake— hearty on the part of Madero, nominal on the part of Orozco. To the crowd looking on, it had all the appearance of sincerity. Great cheers from the crowd. Amity again in Mexico.

But Villa was still in the *carcel,* and there was fear for him. There were rumors and reports related as authentic. Villa had been lined up against a wall and shot that afternoon. There was no more of Villa, the bandit and patriot and thief.

Elfego Baca was in his room—No. 8—at the Zeigler Hotel in El Paso that night when there came a knock and a summons. Colonel Villa wanted to have conversation with Elfego Baca. But Villa was dead, said Mr. Baca. Don't be foolish, said the messenger in polite Spanish. Would Mr. Baca come, as Colonel Villa had requested? But, yes.

They started through the streets of El Paso. At a corner they were stopped by two Villistas. At the next corner they were stopped by two more. At the next corner by an additional two. They finally reached Villa at the entrance to a little known El Paso alley.

"They told me you were killed," said Elfego in astonishment.

Villa waved a bland, disdainful hand as if to say: "Bah! Me killed? By them!"

And the gist of the following conversation was that Villa had certain things he wanted to turn over to Baca for safe-keeping, if he would come to Mexican headquarters next morning at ten o'clock. It would be worth Mr. Baca's while. There were valuables and the like, hinted Villa, and Elfego willingly consented to the trust.

He consented but he never reached the side of Pancho Villa next morning at ten o'clock. The reason being that the American troops had stopped all entrance into Mexico from the American side of the border. By the time Elfego could reach Juarez again, Villa was gone.

From various sources Elfego learned that he was not exactly a prime favorite with Pancho following his failure to land in Juarez on time. Baca always thought that Villa had jewels and money to be turned over, but he was never to know, for the next word he had indirectly from Mr. Villa was that Mr. Villa would be happy to ladle out the sum of $30,000 to get Mr. Baca on the Mexican side of the border. Mr. Villa had a reputation for being rapid with his dislikes.

Mr. Villa also had superior ways of relieving individuals of their possessions. The collections he made on his various raids were of a nature to flood the Villa hacienda to overflowing. It was along this line that Elfego Baca later testified before a committee of Congress.

"So Villa was originally a cattleman, eh?" said Chairman Flood. "Bought and sold cattle, did he?"

"No," said Elfego. "Just sold 'em."

It was this proclivity of Colonel Villa's for what did not belong to him that resulted in his arrest two years later for relieving General Huerta of a blooded stallion valued at $1,000. Villa was lugged off to the jail in Mexico City, but walked out a week or two later with the aid of friendly guards.

It was before the day of Villa's ascendency in Mexico, and Mexico City was not a comfortable place for him. The friends who had got him out of jail were now concerned with getting him out of the city. The few days they kept him under cover were highly uncomfortable days, for Huerta was hot on the trail immediately. It was necessary to get Villa well on his way, and the roads out of Mexico City were guarded by gentlemen less friendly than the guards at the prison.

It resulted in Villa's nearest approach to Christianity. From some mysterious source came the complete garb of a Franciscan Friar, and Pancho was encased within it. Quite piously and thankfully he donned the long brown robe, threw over his shoulders a long gold chain with crucifix, and covered his head with the broad rimmed hat of the order.

Very casually he strolled by Huerta officers who could be assured of rapid promotion by reaching out and nabbing the figure under the priest's robe. There was no nabbing in the city and none at the railroad station where he boarded the train for Juarez. His papers were all of a piece to show that Padre Francisco intended to visit the churches in northern Mexico in a peaceful mission having not the slightest to do with ructions then impending in the bellicose republic.

It was a strange role for the impetuous Pancho Villa, whose morning meal was usually not

complete unless he had ordered the firing squad
to pepper the latest victim of his quest. It was
monkey business for a man who thought as little
of another human life as did Pancho Villa. It was
fairly important to Pancho Villa who thought rather much of his own existence, and took care of it,
despite all tales to the contrary.

On the train during the long drawn out journey from Mexico City to Juarez through the war
torn country, Villa was as demure as a nun on her
first excursion into the world. Patiently he sat
in the dilapidated coach on the train that stopped
every hundred yards for the brakeman to run
ahead and examine the track. Among the passen-
gers he recognized men who would have been
pleased—ay, thankful and elated—to turn his
dangerous form over to Huerta.

Villa was quiet. He was truly god-like, and
retiring, and patient. He fondled the chain which
bore the crucifix. He kept his eyes averted from
the gaze of the vulgarian. On the few occasions
when he was spoken to, he looked past the speaker,
rolled his eyes heavenward, and uttered but one
sound:

"Ah-h!"

It connoted a complete severance from world-
ly cares. It also bespoke a man who had been well
coached and who was aware that if he opened his
mouth for real speech the only thing certain in his
case would be an early morning firing squad.

That trip required the better part of a week, and constituted a strain on the nerves of Pancho Villa. It ended with his entrance into the arms of sympathetic friends at Juarez. Being friends of a nature not often visited by members of the clergy, they were more than a bit put out by the visit of the *padre*. In the excitement—so the story runs—the agitated householders neglected to provide those little touches of hospitality due not only a member of the church but any other respectable visitor.

Upon seeing which, Mr. Pancho Villa uttered the heated words:

"A chair! By the gods, what the hell kind of a dump is this!"

And the good householders fell into a state of joy at sound of the voice coming, as it were, more from below than above in the scale of churchly things. The voice of one only on this whirling sphere—Pancho Villa, who threw off his holy garments, stretched himself in comfort for the first time in many days, and gave his sulphurous opinion on the merits of priestly garb for a real he-man.

When next he arrived in Juarez he came at the head of his own troops hot on the trail of the Huerta contingent. With him was Roberts, a young newspaper man of Santa Fe, New Mexico, who had made a small fortune acting as Villa's representative with the American press. It was

Roberts who brought the message to Elfego Baca that Villa would again enjoy the pleasure of his company. Elfego had not at this time heard of the $30,000 offer, but he had received hints that Pancho was not altogether friendly.

"How does Villa feel toward me?" he asked Roberts.

"Oh, Villa likes you," said Roberts.

"And how about Orozco?" asked Elfego.

"Well, Villa doesn't like Orozco, of course," admitted Roberts.

Orozco and Baca were in close conjunction.

"You go back and tell Villa I'll see him over here any time he wants to," said Elfego. "I'm too busy to get away just now."

"Villa's a pretty busy man, too," Roberts reminded him. "I'm afraid he won't be able to get over."

"Well, I'm sorry," said Elfego.

"Why don't you come over and see Villa?" persisted Roberts.

"Why don't he come over and see me?" said Elfego.

"Well," laughed Roberts. "To be honest, I guess he's afraid somebody would take a pot shot at him."

"Oh, sure!" said Elfego, "but it's all right for me to come over and get shot in the back by Villa. I'll meet him anywhere he wants to, and I don't care how mad he is. But I'm not going over there and let him shoot me from behind. You bring him to the border and give me a chance to look him straight in the face, and I'll talk to him. He's a dirty yellow dog, Roberts, and you know it; go back and tell him I said so. You can tell him also he's a dead Mexican if I ever get near him with a gun.''

Roberts may or may not have returned with the exact message as sent by Elfego Baca. It is enough to know that Villa and Baca never met again. This despite the fact that Villa was many times in the United States—unofficially, of course —and Elfego was often in Mexico—in all defiance of international law. Things were complicated by the further fact that Elfego engineered a coup that resulted in Villa losing one of his muchly beloved Mauser rifles, four of which had been hand tooled for the Mexican leader at a cost of $1,000 apiece.

Villa knew that Elfego Baca had arranged for the gun to be stolen, and was aware of the further fact that Elfego possessed the gun in all defiance of his desire to have it back. Coupled with this desire was the considerable reward of $30,000 which has been spoken of. But Villa was never to have the gun or Elfego Baca.

Mr. Baca thought seriously, however, of collecting the $30,000 and went so far as to arrange the details of a plan whereby he would ostensibly be borne into the presence of Senor Villa in re-

Elfego Baca carrying the gun he had stolen from Pancho
Villa. For which Villa offered a reward of $30,000 for
Elfego, dead or alive.

turn for the money in gold. It had to do with
negotiations which would lead to an exchange of
prisoner Elfego Baca in return for the money of
Villa. Senor Baca was to be transferred, the
money to be collected, and at the same time a
fusillade was to be turned loose that would result
in the escape of Elfego Baca. The plot reached
the point where everything was ready but the
$30,000 of Bandit Villa. Things in Mexico were
progressing at too rapid a pace to allow Mr. Villa
to pause and consider the pleasure of possessing
the person of Elfego Baca, and the thing fell
through.

CHAPTER ELEVEN

GENERAL SALAZAR ESCAPES FROM JAIL

It was soon after that Elfego was hired by Huerta to act as his American representative and to defend General Jose Ynez Salazar, who had been interned by the American government after the battle of Ojinaga.

The case of Salazar is one of the most interesting, from an American standpoint, arising out of all the Mexican trouble. Salazar was originally a Mexican but had spent many years in mining camps of New Mexico and Arizona. When the Mexican rumpus started he offered his services to Madero and was commissioned commander of a squad. Later under Huerta he became Brigadier General and eventually commander of a division. He was active in this role at the battle of Ojinaga when the Huerta forces were crushed and forced to flee over the border into the United States for safety. Once over they were interned by the American Government for violation of neutrality. Salazar escaping at the same time, according to testimony given against him later, was arrested at Sanderson, Texas, January 17, 1914, and taken immediately to Fort Bliss at El Paso.

It was a message from there to Elfego Baca at Socorro that brought our hero into the case.

Elfego arrived at Fort Bliss and went immediately to see General Scott, the commandant. Coud he, as attorney for Salazar, have a chance to confer with his client? He most emphatically could not! Not that General Scott gave three whoops who General Salazar talked to, but the big boys in Washington, for some reason, did. Every prominent lawyer in El Paso had already been there on the same errand, but the war department was immovable. It might be against all justice and ethics, but Salazar was not to be seen by anybody.

Would General Scott have objection if a further attempt was made to sway the war department? Not at all. It made no slightest difference to General Scott and Elfego fashioned a telegram to Senator A. B. Fall in Washington setting out the facts of the case and asking that his influence be used with the war department so that General Salazar might have benefit of counsel in his predicament. The message was sent at eleven o'clock in the morning and Mr. Baca said he would wait right where he was for an answer.

He waited until noon in an ante-room to General Scott's office, and was still there patiently sitting when the General went out for lunch. He was there at two o'clock under the not too friendly gaze of underofficers who were not overly enamoured of the cause for which General Salazar stood. He was there at three o'clock, unworried, unbothered, persistent, when his name was announced from General Scott's office and he was ushered in.

"I didn't think you had a chance," said the General, throwing a telegram across the desk. It gave permission for one Elfego Baca to have words with one General Jose Ynez Salazar, late of the Huerta forces and now reluctant guest of the United States army.

Mr. Baca was taken out and admitted through the barbed wire entanglement which confined Salazar. In going through the gate he saw three or four American guards fondling their rifles in a careless way which bespoke disaster for whomever disaster overtook. They laughed lightly, did these cheerful guards, and continued to prime their guns and play jestfully with the triggers and point them accidently in the direction of the tent containing Salazar.

Mr. Baca stopped where he was and retreated in good order. He headed back for the office of General Scott.

"What's the matter?" asked the General.

"Nothing," said Elfego, "except that there's going to be a Fourth of July celebration down there at the gate and I don't want to be the sky rocket."

The frolicksome guards were removed and Elfego went back to have words with his client.

It was a great business for Elfego. He re-

General Salazar a prisoner at Fort Bliss, El Paso.

ceived a fee of $25,000 and expense money amounting to $3,500. For Salazar it must have been a tiresome affair. From Fort Bliss he was taken to Fort Wingate near Gallup in New Mexico. With him went the remnants of the Huerta force that had fled across the border into the United States after the route of Ojinaga. Men, women and children. The Mexican fights as he lives. Where he goes, goes also the family.

They fled from Chihuahua to Ojinaga, lock, stock and barrel. Perched on box cars, strung out along dusty, hot roads. They came now to Fort Wingate under close guard, and prepared to go into camp for life, if need be.

There is little to be remembered of the prolonged period there. The one thing that sticks in the recollection of New Mexico visitors to the camp is that the Mexicans had a band of surpassing excellence.

It was a band of rag tail and bob tail. Its members were without question the dirtiest, most ragged, deplorable set of humans ever gathered in one group. But they could make music as sweetly as the Herald angels. They *could* make it, but they wouldn't unless on order from General Salazar.

It was a strange triumph of discipline. They were imprisoned, poverty stricken, and faced with a long stay in the hoose-gow. In addition they were wild for music by the time Sunday straggled

around. But there was no music unless Salazar
issued a written order. Nary a horn tooted, nary
a clarinet squeaked, nary a bow rasped across the
belly of a bull fiddle without the word of Jose
Ynez Salazar.

The case of Salazar dragged on. Elfego
sought to have him released under writ of habeas
corpus. Salazar's affidavits and answers in this
proceeding were of such nature that the Grand
Jury at Santa Fe on October 9, 1914, indicted Salazar for perjury. Prior to this Elfego Baca had
appeared in Washington before the State Department and the War Department on behalf of Salazar. While at Washington he had also testified
at a House hearing into the causes of the Mexican
imbroglio and the possibility of American recognition of Huerta.

In the meantime because of rumors of plots,
Salazar was returned to Fort Bliss where he could
be better watched. It was to answer the charge of
perjury that Salazar was brought to the Bernalillo County jail at Albuquerque. He entered on
November 16, 1914 and left for good on November
20, 1914, four days later. He left in one of the
most sensational jail deliveries in Southwestern
history. The reverberations of it are still bound-
ing back and forth in our part of the country.

It is well to stop at this point and take stock.
The generally credited story of the escape of Salazar is so different from the true story that an

explanation is necessary. The true story is now for the first time being told in print. It is even to this day known to only a few outside the circle involved.

It is known definitely that on the night of November 20, 1914, at 9:30 o'clock, two masked men overpowered jailer Charles Armijo, bound and gagged him, and released General Salazar from his cell on the second floor of the jail.

It was thought then and is still held as an undisputed fact by the greater part of the citizenry of Albuquerque that the whole plot was engineered by Elfego Baca in conjunction with officials of Bernalillo County. Elfego Baca; Manuel Vigil, district attorney of Bernalillo County; Trinidad C. De Baca, state game warden; the jailer, and lesser figures were tried for conspiracy against the Government of the United States. They were acquitted.

To start with, there was a phone call for help from a street north of town. A lady was in great distress. Help! The guard bolted off to the rescue, leaving Armijo alone guarding the jail. What happened to Armijo is history.

The theory is that Salazar was met by a motor car, taken to the ranch of Celestino Otero, near Albuquerque, and secreted to Mexico after the first hullabaloo of the search had died down. Manuel Vigil, district attorney, was in Gallup, 166 miles away, at the time of the jail break. Elfego

Baca was in the company of the chief deputy U. S. Marshal Galusha and of George Craig at the Graham saloon in Albuquerque at the time of the escape of Salazar. But it was thought that Baca and Vigil had arranged the details of the jail delivery and were carefully establishing alibis at the time Salazar made his getaway. This is the story believed almost unanimously by people now living in Albuquerque, despite the verdict of the jury in the conspiracy case.

The actual story is quite a bit different and many times more thrilling.

The Huerta forces hiding in and about El Paso had watched the Salazar case from the first with the greatest of interest. There had been fire-eating members of the Huerta contingent who had been in favor of attempting Salazar's rescue from Fort Wingate and later from Fort Bliss. They had been rudely over-ruled by Huerta and Orozco, who had confidence in Elfego Baca. That confidence was in a fair way to being realized when the federal court sitting in Santa Fe granted Salazar a writ of habeas corpus. It seemed that the affair was over, and that Salazar was finally to have his freedom.

It developed, however, that a writ of habeas corpus in war time was a different thing than the same writ at other moments. Orders were received from Washington that writ or no writ Salazar was to be held. The federal district at-

Left to right: Elfego Baca; General Salazar; J. B. McGuinnes,
Mr. Baca's secretary. At Fort Bliss before coming to
Albuquerque for trial.

torney in New Mexico informed the court of the
government's determination, and Salazar continued to languish.

The fire-eaters of the Huerta following came
to the fore with a rush when this report reached
El Paso. They were joined by every other member of the contingent, and Huerta personally gave
the word that Salazar was to be taken from the
Bernalillo county jail by ruse if possible, by force
if necessary.

The jail break was planned with extreme care.
Two operatives of the Huerta secret service were
despatched to Albuquerque to plot out the city in
detail.   One was a beautiful senorita whose tri-
umphs had brought her to the pinnacle of secret
service work in Mexico.   As an adventuress who
stepped almost bodily out of such romances as are
indited so successfully by E. Phillips Oppenheim
and others, Senorita Margherita had been the
backbone of the Huerta movement on several
occasions when a carefully dropped word in the
midst of the enemy's camp had meant life for the
Huerta forces. She had operated in Mexico City
at times when a whisper of suspicion would have
meant her life. She had dined in public with officers of the Villa forces.   She was—and is—
genuinely beautiful, and clever in a way most
pleasing to rough men.

She came to Albuquerque with her male partner and gathered every detail that might be use-

ful to the men who were to come for actual operations. She made a map of Albuquerque which could be used to this day. Not only was it accurate, but it was direct and to the point. It showed the position of the jail and of the railroad station and of the streets leading between the two. She also arranged for the phone call—arranged, in short, where she could have the security of making the call in person. She brought food and presents to prisoners in the jail other than General Salazar. She arrived in Albuquerque and made visits to the jail, in fact, long before General Salazar even arrived there from Fort Bliss.

Things simultaneously began to move in the El Paso sector. They were helped by the fact that at the time there was a great shortage of labor in the Colorado beet fields, and tempting offers were being made to Mexican laborers of the Southwest. In addition to good wages—almost unbelievable wages in Mexican eyes—the workers were given round trip railroad tickets. The beet picking season was short, the laborers were assured of good wages, and were given in advance a ticket back home. It was paradise to the workmen, and luck incarnate for the Huerta conspirators.

From El Paso, disguised as Mexican laborers, went the party that was to free Salazar. Headed by General Pascual Orozco, the same rough Orozco who had captured Juarez from Madero, they proceeded to Colorado. In the party were General

Jose de La Luz Blanco, General Francisco Castro, General Luis Fuentes, brother-in-law of Huerta; General Roque Gomez; General Manuel Landa, General Sebo Lopez, General Alberto Quiroz, also brother-in-law of Huerta, General S. F. Rivero and Colonel Alphonso Porras.

The names will probably mean nothing to you, and you will have a few giggles over the misfortune of Porras, who was permitted to belong to the party while yet suffering under the poor ignominious title of Colonel. But your laughs will be wasted. The members who started for the beet fields of Colorado with the intention of getting Salazar out of jail in Albuquerque were the backbone of the entire Huerta movement. The successive Mexican revolutions were always considered more or less of a joke in the United States. Which is not to say of course that they were anything but the most important happenings possible to a Mexican. The successful attempt to release Salazar from bondage was much as if Generals Joffre, Foch and Lyautey had formed a raiding party during the war to secure the person of, say, General Petain who happened to be in a Berlin prison. The capture of the Mexican generals in an effort to release General Salazar would have meant the immediate collapse of the Huerta effort.

At any rate, the Mexican generals' outing party continued on to Colorado and stayed there a period of two days. They left then on their round trip tickets and came back to Albuquerque at 7:30 on the night of November 20. Quietly enough they had supper with friends who had been awaiting them, and conferred with the beautiful maiden and her secret service male friend who had done the preliminary work. The map of Albuquerque was gone over carefully. Street corners were alloted to various members of the party for surveillance. The various members of the party were armed to the teeth. They were in a strange town and they knew it. They also knew that mercy would be the last thing they might expect if a slip up should reveal them for what they were.

The train arrived from Colorado at seventy-thirty at night. The train would leave for El Paso at 10:15 the same night. They ate a leisurely supper and strolled out to inspect the town. As they peeked in at the door of the Graham Bar, they saw Elfego Baca in steady and loving conversation with his friends. It was a question of gulp, gulp, a bit of conversation, and "Now, *you* have one on *me*." They were having a pleasant, easy evening in the Graham Saloon.

It was a warm November evening in Albuquerque, and things moved at the same steady pace as has always characterized the metropolis of New Mexico. Good citizens and their wives walked down town to the movies or sat at home under the reading lamp in more or less dispas-

sionate interest over the doings of the armies of
the world war.

The gay dogs of the city lounged leisurely
through the swinging doors of the saloons, and
paused to converse with compatriots on the char--
acteristic mildness of the Albuquerque November.
There was in the air no hint of the massacre that
could quite easily fall upon the city of Albuquerque should some of the more alert burghers discover the identity of the "Spanish-American" gentlemen who rested easily against the telephone posts
at various of the principal street corners.

Promptly at 9:30 the telephone rang at the
Bernalillo County jail and the female voice of
great distress came over the wire. Mrs. Chavez
needed help immediately. Mrs. Chavez at 1012
North Twelfth Street. A man was breaking in the
house! Oh! Oh! Would the jailer come at once.
Wouldn't he *please*, please, come at once!

The guard stood not on the order of his going. A lady was in distress. Enough. He left
Charley Armijo alone in the jail.

Mr. Charles Armijo had scarcely time to think
of his responsibilities when a stern voice coming
from a window behind him in the jailer's office
ordered him to throw them up and keep them up.
The next Mr. Armijo knew he was being seized
from behind in any but a tender manner. A gag
was over his mouth, his arms were being pinned
and he was being relieved of his guns and of his

keys. There were, as Mr. Armijo discovered after he was finally tied to a chair, two masked men of belligerent nature. To prove their earnestness and sincerity they presented Mr. Armijo with several resounding socks on the jaw when he attempted to remonstrate at their levity in the face of the law.

While one of them stayed in the office to keep Mr. Armijo company, the other departed with the keys in his hand as if he had been living in the jail all his natural life. He went along the corridor, up the stairs to the second floor, and soon returned with General Salazar. There was no commotion about it. The masked man opened the door of the General's cell, and the General, all prepared, walked out. It was this familiarity with the accommodations of the jail that made local officers certain that the job was pulled off by men on the inside. Which was no more true than any other general surmises of our highly touted guardians of the nation's safety.

Taking a few more pokes at the helpless Mr. Armijo as a parting gesture, the two masked men and General Salazar crawled through the open window of the jailer's office and were enveloped in the security of a waiting motor car. They then proceeded to drive straight down lighted Central Avenue, the principal thoroughfare in the city of Albuquerque, New Mexico, U. S. A. There are even tales to the effect that in passing the Graham

Bar, the General was so carried away by elation as to lean far out of the moving motor car to wave good-bye to his attorney, Elfego Baca.

"Adios, mi Abogado."

The signal was given to the generals guarding the street corners. When the car was once past unmolested, the generals were free to desert their posts. They did so, coming down Central Avenue toward the railroad station on the alert for any monkey shines that might disturb the triumphal procession of General Jose Ynez Salazar. It is not to say that the Mexican gentry would have gotten away with it if their presence had been detected, but it is a certainty that there would have been tragedy in Albuquerque that night if the plot had been discovered. There would have been Albuquerque shooting and Mexican shooting and the result would not have been pleasant for those concerned.

The party boarded the El Paso train at 10:05 and was dragged away from Albuquerque at 10:15. It was 10:20 when the guard returned to the jail after failing to find the distressed lady. He found at the jail, however, a distressed Charley Armijo, who was accused later of bashing himself in the face in an effort to throw suspicion from the real conspirators. There was alarm. There was hullabaloo. It was a great, exciting occasion, and Elfego Baca was at once the center of it. Elfego Baca was the center of it in the sense that the pursuers of Jose Ynez Salazar shadowed Mr. Elfego Baca with the thought that what he did would reveal where Jose Ynez was. The shadowing revealed nothing that night but the fact that Elfego Baca was sleepy and was going home to bed. He was followed home to bed, and his house was watched all night with the thought that he would become less weary and decide to decamp for the scene of the Salazar hiding place.

The remainder of the active population was following buggy tracks and automobile tracks throughout the length and breadth of Bernalillo County. Many a modest Spanish-American homestead was wakened rudely by the hue and cry of an indignant posse. Many a household was routed into the cool night air because of the far from original notion of the pursuers that Salazar might be hiding under a treacherous Spanish-American bed. No Salazar was found, for Salazar at the moment was on the El Paso train bound for the safety of the Mexican border.

The only hitch in the proceedings was at Belen, the first stop out of Albuquerque, when the conductor of the train made motions to visit the telegraph office with nobody knew what tidings. To be on the safe side, General Orozco spoke soft words to the railroad gentleman while poking a six shooter significantly in his ribs. There was no further confab or offer of confab with the telegrapher. The Orozco-Salazar party left the train

The mysterious and unknown adventuress who laid the
groundwork for the escape of General Salazar from the
Albuquerque jail.

at the little station of La Tuna, four miles this side of El Paso at seven o'clock next morning and disappeared across the border without molestation.

Meanwhile the house of Elfego Baca in Albuquerque was being watched by amateur sleuths. When the good attorney arose next morning and proceeded to depart in horse and buggy with his wife and a neighbor for a trip to friends in the Sandia mountains near the city, he was accompanied at a distance by the same anxious men who had been doubtful of his fatigue the night before.

They shadowed Mr. Baca for weeks and finally tried him in court with just as good results as usual; to-wit, none.

CHAPTER TWELVE

HUERTA DIES

In El Paso, as the American representative of Huerta, Elfego enjoyed the emoluments due a man who would, if Huerta triumphed, become a power in the republic to the South. He considered offers that would have made him a millionaire in case of Huerta's recognition. Famous among the offers was one for the sole concession to the gambling rights in Mexico City. A casino would be built at a cost of five million dollars and Mexico City would become the nearest rival to Monte Carlo on the face of the globe. The plan was backed by men of consequence in the United States. For getting the concession, Mr. Baca was to receive the sum of $50,000. He talked the matter over with Huerta and Orozco, who saw nothing wrong with the idea, and agreed to take it under consideration pending the outcome of events in Mexico.

A second concession was to have been given a firm of Chicago packers who would have the sole packing rights in the Mexican State of Chihuahua. Elfego was much in the same position as "Red" Grange on his famous New York trip. There were to be no chocolate candies or cigars named after Elfego Baca, but he could have taken his choice of a dozen offers for concessions that would have made his fortune.

Consequently Mr. Baca was doing all mortal man could to further the interests of Mr. Huerta. Things had progressed to the point where General Orelas in command of the garrison in Juarez was ready to listen to reason if the proper inducements were forthcoming. It took only the modest sum of $30,000 to affect the public morals of General Orelas, who had agreed to have a white flag of surrender ready as soon as the Huerta forces had fired a volley and made motions toward an attack on Juarez. The money was finally ready, the Huerta forces had taken proper precautions to make certain that General Orelas was not double-crossing them, and all lacking was the command of Huerta himself, who was returning to El Paso from a prolonged visit *incognito* in the eastern part of the United States. He had rallied financial support that had become shaky, and was on his way back to Mexico to conquer the country for good and all.

Within ten miles of El Paso he was arrested by American officers and taken from the train as a captive. Once in El Paso, he was placed under constant surveillance, and held a prisoner of war, on the charge of having violated the neutrality of the United States.

It was the end of the Huerta movement and the end of Huerta himself. Addicted to the absinthe habit, of which he took forty or fifty drinks a day in a half cup of coffee, the former strong man of Mexico wilted away. He sipped his absinthe, cogitated on plans which he knew had little chance of fulfillment, thought of steps in the past that might have made all the difference between success and failure, and saw his world of domination fall in ruins about him.

It was a sad day for many when Huerta died. It was a sad day for the American bankers who had supplied money and arms with the understanding either that their old holdings would be restored to them and that they would have protection for them in the future or that they were to have new concessions that could not help making them fabulously wealthy. It was a sad day for the Mexican emigres who made up the forlorn retinue of Huerta. With them it was a question of keeping outside the clutches of the United States Government which had become very touchy in regard to Mexicans bouncing back and forth across the border or they could return across the Rio Grande definitely and take the chance of running full tilt into a vindictive Villa firing squad.

For Elfego Baca the choice was easy. He simply went back to Socorro and dismissed from his mind the thoughts of dominance and wealth that had been lingering there. His days of international intrigue were over. His days of bribing garrisons, of arranging finances, of protecting liti-

General Huerta, one-time President of Mexico, for whom
Elfego Baca acted as American representative.

gants, of appearing before Washington depart-
ments in support of his clients' interests, were
done. They were finished, and Elfego was a New
Mexican again for life.

CHAPTER THIRTEEN

Elfego Kills Celestino Otero

An aftermath to the Salazar case seemed inevitable, and it came with the death in El Paso of Celestino Otero as a result of a gun in the hands of Elfego Baca. Otero will be remembered as one of the alleged conspirators in the Salazar escape, to whose ranch Salazar was said to have been taken after the jail break, according to the story of the government in the prosecution of the conspirators. It was a story not believed by the jury in the case, and it is a story that cannot possibly be the truth if Salazar was taken from Albuquerque as previously related in this history.

The impression still lingers heavily in Albuquerque that the death of Otero was a plot meant to silence one member of the gang of conspirators who had the temerity to ask additional reward for his participation. It is still quite generally believed that Elfego Baca and his friend Dr. Romero, of El Paso, deliberately "framed" Otero, who was thought to have been overly insistent on being paid what was due him for his part in the Salazar escape.

According to this theory—which has been recounted before—Otero had allowed his ranch to be used as a refuge for Salazar after his flight from the Bernalillo County jail. Salazar was alleged to have remained in hiding at the Otero ranch until after the first hubbub had blown over. If this is true there can then be no truth in the story of Salazar's escape given herein.

"Oh, Elfego," say his detractors with a shrug of disgust. "How can you ever hope to convict him of anything with Mexican juries always sitting on the case."

To which Elfego Baca can answer with the names of the jurors at El Paso. M. H. Lemen, William Meisel, T. M. White, S. C. G. Reum, B. P. Klerner, William Alberts, J. A. Chipps, Albert Cockrill, H. Van Bruggen, Sam Hill, Kernel Lewis, and C. N. Bassett, foreman. Everything, you will notice, but an ancient Castilian or a modern Mexican name. A typical high-class jury, forsooth, and one which walked from the court room to the jury room, took one oral poll of the jury, and returned with a verdict of "not guilty!", a procedure which took in all the vast total of five minutes!

But to proceed to the story of the Otero trouble as given by Elfego Baca.

Baca and Dr. Romero, coming out of the lobby of the Paso del Norte Hotel in El Paso, were accosted by Celestino Otero, who wished to have private conversation with Elfego.

"Come over here to the corner of the lobby and I'll talk to you," said Elfego.

"No," said Otero. "I want to talk to you alone."

"Well, we can go back upstairs to my room," said Elfego. "You won't mind for a minute, will you, Dr. Romero?"

"Not at all," said the Doctor.

But Otero seemed to need even more privacy. He suggested after a pause that Elfego meet him at the cafe of Marcil Andugo near the international bridge.

This ordinarily would have sounded suspicious to him, says Elfego. But by a coincidence it happened that just two days before he had visited the cafe of Andugo with the idea of collecting from him a $500 debt left owing from a law suit in which Elfego had defended Andugo. At that time Andugo had promised Elfego part payment and said he was expecting some money in a few days, at which time he would get in touch with Elfego. It flashed through Elfego's head at Otero's words that the visit might have to do with the repayment of the debt.

"That's perfectly all right," said Elfego. "We can go right down there in Dr. Romero's car. Eh, Doctor?"

"Perfectly agreeable to me," said Dr. Romero and led the way out of the lobby.

"A friend of mine has a car parked around on another street," said Otero. "You go on down and I'll meet you there."

Dr. Romero and Elfego started off. It was Sunday, and the Andugo cafe was practically deserted at that time of afternoon. They inquired of the bartender for the whereabouts of Mr. Andugo.

"Mr. Andugo never comes down on Sunday," said the bartender. "He always goes out riding with his wife and children."

"Hum!" thought Elfego. "Then it couldn't have been about the money Andugo owes me."

Otero had not shown up, and for the first time suspicion began to enter the mind of Elfego.

"Let's get out of here," he said to Dr. Romero, and they hastened back to the car, still without catching sight of Otero.

They drove up the street to where the railroad crosses Santa Fe street, and there they were halted by a shifting train. The train blocked the roadway, but had cleared the crossing to a point where one side of the sidewalk was clear. The Romero car was, of course, blocked. As they stood there waiting, Elfego saw Otero and several companions come over the crossing along the sidewalk. They saw Elfego in the car and approached at once.

"What's the matter," said Otero. "Why didn't you wait?"

"Now, look here," said Elfego, suddenly confirmed in his suspicions by the tone of Otero's voice. "I'm damned tired of all this fooling

around. What do you want with me? Come on!
What do you want?''

And he got out of the door of the car on the
side away from Otero and started around the rear
of the machine to accost him. As he made the
turn to face Otero, a shot from Otero's gun cut
across the groin of Elfego and half whirled him
in a position to face Otero. It was enough. It
was the last shot from Otero. Two rapid bullets
struck the heart of Otero a quarter of an inch
apart and killed him instantly.

Elfego didn't wait to discover the consequences of his act. He got back into Dr. Romero's car
and drove to the home of his attorney. From
there he called the office of the chief of police of
El Paso.

''This is Elfego Baca,'' he said. ''I've just
killed a man down on Santa Fe street. I'm waiting over here at Armijo's house for you. Come
yourself. If you send some fresh cop who tries to
get rough with me, you know what'll happen to
him. I'll wait here for you.''

His arrest and trial were events that stirred
the Southwest, as every action of his seems to
have done. His attorneys charged that Celestino
Otero had been promised $8,000 by a mem-
ber of a powerful family in the state of New Mexico if he would proceed to El Paso and ''get'' Elfego. It will be remembered that Elfego's first
escapade in getting his father out of the Los Lun-

as jail had been due—he always charged—to the
action of this powerful family, in getting his father in. The feud started then had not abated
through the years, and had flamed more brightly
than ever after the mysterious death of one of
their members and the veiled charges growing out
of it. The charges were general and Elfego, in
the circumstances, was not one to be in the background. At the time he owned a weekly Spanish
paper in which he hesitated not the slightest to
give his opinion of how the gentleman came to his
sudden end.

Whatever the truth of it all, the El Paso jury
acquitted Elfego almost as soon as they could get
from the court room to the jury room and back
again.

There is a dubiously truthful story which for
years has gone the rounds in New Mexico in regard to one of the numerous murder trials of
Elfego. Elfego himself laughs at it, but it is interesting enough to give here.

Elfego, was, as usual, on trial for murder and
things were going badly with his case. He had
killed a man in cold blood, so the story goes, and
he was at a loss for a line of defense. The deed
had been witnessed by a dozen people, all of them
ready to testify that Elfego was guilty. On the
defense side there was nobody—nobody but Elfego. Elfego gave his attorney but one order.

"Keep this case going for two weeks."

"But . . . ." began the bewildered avocat.

"No matter," said Elfego. "I tell you to keep it going. I don't care how you do it. Just keep it going."

Following which Elfego wheeled his chair to face the jury box and, singling out one juror a day, brought to bear on him such a piercing, belligerent, threatening eye as has not been seen on the entire western continent more than half a dozen times in all history. It was a penetrating eye that came out from beneath lowering, bushy eyebrows and threw a stiletto-like gleam into the object of its attention.

The attorney in the meantime was doing his best to drag out the case. It was a tough job, but Elfego's eye was also turned on him if he showed signs of wilting. It was a matter of hanging on to the witnesses for the prosecution as long as the irritated judge would permit. The examination was something like this:

"Hum! Hu-um! Now, eh . . . . You say you were . . . . Hu-um! Well, let me see now . . . You say you were standing on the sidewalk directly . . . . It was directly, wasn't it? . . . . Hu-um . . . directly behind Elfego Baca when . . . . Hu-um! Are you certain it was directly behind . . . .?

"Ask the question," demands the judge.

"Well, you were standing on the sidewalk directly behind Elfego Baca when . . . . . "

"*Si!*" answers the weary witness. "*Si!* I was standing there and I saw it."

"How old are you?" asks the lawyer for Mr. Baca.

"Forty-six," answers the witness.

"Any children?"

"Yes, five."

"How many boys?"

"Three."

"Then you have two girls?"

"Yes, certainly."

"Anybody in your family ever have small-pox?"

"What has smallpox got to do with this case?" demands the judge rudely.

"Your honor," says the attorney, drawing himself up with what passes in a court of law as dignity. "Your honor, it is my intention to show that this man is no fit witness because . . . . . ."

"Get on to the shooting," counsels the judge. "Let the smallpox alone."

Elfego was meanwhile keeping up his ocular barrage on individual members of the jury. With some half a day was sufficient. With others it took two days. All was helped by testimony of the one defense witness. Said witness being—according to the story—Elfego's brother, Francisco, who looked equally as hard-boiled as Elfego, and who had been called merely as a witness to the good reputation previously sustained by his famous brother. Said testimony for good reputation having to do with the fact that in all previous murder trials, Elfego had been freed by the jury. Francisco in addition had the following bit of testimony to offer:

He gave it as his opinion that Elfego was undoubtedly the best shot with a pistol in all these United States with the sole exception of one other —that being himself, Francisco. Elfego, testified Francisco, could hit a jack rabbit from a distance of fifty yards while riding full tilt on the back of a plunging cow-pony. This was excellent, but it was a well established fact that Francisco could achieve the same feat at a distance of *one hundred yards!* Francisco was, to put it modestly, some shot with a pistol or a rifle, and he loved his brother very dearly. It was a question in his mind, Francisco allowed it to be learned, whether he could ever again bear friendly feeling toward any man who dealt harshly with his brother, Elfego. With these words, Francisco turned to look fully and significantly at the jury.

There is no use to go on with the story. The judge did everything but order the jury to bring in a verdict of "Guilty," and the jury was out ten minutes and brought in a verdict of "Acquittal" So goes the story, at any rate, and there is no insistence that it be credited.

CHAPTER FOURTEEN

ELFEGO MEETS MARY GARDEN

If a personal word may again be pardoned at this juncture, we should like to make mention of the first time we had the pleasure of seeing Mr. Baca. It must be understood that he has always been a figure of great interest in New Mexico and El Paso no matter what his fortunes might be at any given moment. There have always been tales enough about him to make it certain that he will be noticed, whether or not he is loved. At the time we first saw him we knew of him solely by a reputation not overly favorable. The idea of inditing his life deeds was farthest from our thoughts. In truth, in view of his reputation, we should have been more than ordinarily perturbed had anybody suggested the idea.

It happened that we were drawn from Albuquerque to El Paso by the fact that the Chicago Grand Opera company was to give performances of "Tosca" and "Carmen" at the latter city. Raisa, Rimini and Edward Johnson were to sing in "Tosca" and Mary Garden, Muratore and Baklanoff in "Carmen". It was an event in Southwestern musical history, and we were early on the ground. We were at the hotel when the opera company landed from San Antonio. At the time

Miss Garden was not only leading prima donna of the company, but director as well.

On the afternoon of the same day we went over to Juarez, as was then and perhaps still is the custom of visitors to El Paso. All gambling at the moment was centered in the Tivoli. It was a huge wooden structure, and all gambling in Juarez was confined to it by order of the Mexican government, which was being paid handsomely for the concession. It contained every form of gambling that we have ever heard of, though we profess no expertness in the matter. There was one large room for keno, and another which contained roulette wheels, and tables for faro and poker and black jack and monte and solo and a half a dozen others we did not recognize.

During our course of wandering through the latter room we came upon Miss Garden before a roulette wheel. With her were Muratore and his beautiful wife, Lina Cavaleria, and others of the Chicago company. They were having a time which could only be described as jolly. At moments when Miss Garden happened to strike "straight up"— and it occurred twice while we watched—the scene threatened to become riotous. Now, if there was one thing that the management of the Tivoli did not encourage, it was revelry. The dealers of faro looked up with a frown and players at the stud games turned about in their chairs to see what all the fuss was about.

Mary Garden, famous opera star, on the steps of the Tivoli at Juarez, with Elfego Baca (left) when he was head bouncer at that noted gambling hall.

It was then that a rotund gentleman of smiling countenance and a black moustache came down the room and paused at the rear of the group about Miss Garden. He paused only for a second and then elbowed his way through to where Miss Garden was playing, placing chips on the red and on the first dozen and on the numbered squares.

"Hello!" he said heartily to Miss Garden, and beamed on her. In truth, his eyes twinkled, but no self respecting author would dare admit such a fact in these latter sophisticated days.

"Hello!" said Miss Garden, doubtfully, not quite certain how to meet this newest form of flirtation.

"Go right ahead," said the man. "I'm just the chief bouncer here. Ask your party to be a little less noisy, but don't stop."

This seemed to strike Miss Garden as being fair enough, and she gave signs of saying so.

"I'm Mary Garden," she said, and reached out her hand.

"I'm Elfego Baca," he said, just as confidently, and took it.

That was as far as the story went in our presence. It struck us at the time that Elfego Baca had not the slightest idea who Mary Garden was and that Mary Garden was equally ill informed as to the significance of Elfego Baca. In looking back at it, it occurs to us that the thrills on that occasion belong almost entirely to us. We were almost as interested in seeing the famous Elfego in the flesh as we were in watching the great Mary at play.

Later when we came to write this book, we asked Mr. Baca about it.

"Oh, the singing lady," he said. "She was nice. Were you there that day? We were together all day. I showed her Juarez, and she made me go back with her to the hotel in El Paso. She gave me a ticket for the show, but I didn't like it. You know, all that hollering around. I like the Mexican string bands better. Here, wait a minute . . . . "

He rummaged around his desk and brought out a picture. It showed Miss Garden and himself and several others on the steps of the Tivoli.

"That's Revilla," he said, pointing to the man on the left of Miss Garden. "He was one of the bosses at the Tivoli. He and Rebia and Lopez and Asteca paid $168,000 a month in gold, Mexican, for the gambling concession. That was about $84,000 a month American. I was in charge of the police force."

Next to his $25,000 fee for defending General Salazar it was the best money Elfego ever made. He had fourteen men under him and was paid $750 a month salary, was given his room and board free, and was furnished with an automobile and chauffeur. He was there because of his reputation with a pistol, and it was the policy of Messrs. Revilla, Rebia, Lopez and Asteca to let the fact of his presence be known to the world. His duties accordingly were light.

The Tivoli was a great establishment. Mr. Baca's work started every morning at eleven, when he superintended the paying off of the help for their work of the day before. The payroll for dealers, police and other workers was in the neighborhood of $4,500 a day. Mr. Baca promptly at eleven every morning pocketed $25 as his share of the proceeds. The dealers worked from eleven till midnight, when the international bridge closed.

It was part of Elfego's job to keep an eye on the dealers and see that they checked in the money they handled. In addition to the police force there was a corps of stool pigeons who played in the games and chummed with the dealers in an effort to trip them up in their graft. At the Tivoli there were two complete lighting systems. Attempts at a raid were made by cutting off the juice, throwing the building in darkness and making away with the money on the tables. It was tried three times during the regime of Elfego Baca, but was frustrated by the second lighting system which flooded the gambling rooms before a move could be made. It was at such moments at this when Elfego earned his pay. It was a time for steady nerves, and the guns of himself and his fourteen men were trained on the gambling tables the instant a false move was made. It was a question of protecting money above everything else at the Tivoli, and when Mr. Baca eventually resigned his position he left with the knowledge that no raid had been a success during his tenure of office.

With precautions what they were at the Tivoli, it might be supposed that raids were more often failures than not. On the contrary, before the advent of Elfego Baca the gang headed by Numero Ocho—Number Eight—had made a practice of it. Numero Ocho was the leader of the Juarez underworld, lower than which it is impossible to imagine life going. He was a tough bird of ruling force in an atmosphere where tough birds flourished. He had made life miserable for Messrs. Revilla, Rebia, Lopez and Asteca prior to the coming of Elfego Baca, and it was suspected that Numero Ocho had the backing of the Juarez police as well as being blessed with inherent toughness.

With a concession cost of $84,000 a month American gold added to a daily overhead for salaries of $4,500 and the additional expenses of rent and amounts spread at the proper places for political reasons, there was little joy in the lives of Messrs. Revilla, Rebia, Lopez and Asteca when Numero Ocho and his outfit developed a habit of dashing in and carrying off the winnings at the tables. It made it even harder on the half witted American tourist who persisted in bucking a game which was faced by that overhead, but Messrs. Revilla, Rebia, Lopez and Asteca were not overcome with remorse on this same ground when their thoughts turned, as they did frequently, to their woes.

Numero Ocho knew of Elfego Baca's arrival almost before the gentleman arrived. He was not long in bringing the tidings to Elfego's ears that his presence was not desired and that any funny business on his part would result in bringing down upon his head the wrath of the entire efficient Numero Ocho organization. It was not a pleasant welcome, but then Elfego was not obsessed with the idea that any such honor was due him for anything he had hitherto accomplished during his lifetime. He knew Number Eight by reputation and was not unduly impressed by a character who felt it best to be known by a number rather than a good decent name.

In the immemorial manner of rough cookies, Numero Ocho let it be known what he would do to Elfego Baca if he ever got near him. Elfego waited patiently, and even sent out couriers to let Ocho know where he might be located. When that was of no avail, Elfego started out to find Numero Ocho. It has been a lifetime custom of Mr. Baca's. His philosophy has always been that when trouble threatened you, the only sane thing was to go and meet it. So he started out in quest of Ocho. He hunted him high and he hunted him low, and he finally discovered him in the cellar which passed as Ocho's headquarters. Ocho was surrounded by his gang and in the heart of his kingdom.

"Which one is Ocho?" said Elfego. "I'm Elfego Baca."

Whereupon he walked across the room and slapped Numero Ocho very neatly on the side of the mouth and caught him with a left hook to the stomach. He finished by slapping—not hitting—Ocho twice more and kicking him severely in the rear when he turned to flee. It was all over in a few moments, and Elfego covered the Ocho gang with his guns while he made them a parting speech. It had to do with his contempt for Numero Ocho and anybody who subscribed to his policies, and delivered warning of what would happen to any of them found in the vicinity of the Tivoli.

We have hesitated to relate the latter part of this story although we have received it from a sound source. To one who knows the temperament of Elfego Baca, it seems the most natural thing in the world; to others, it may smack a bit of Frank Merriwell. Mr. Baca, to this day, makes it a habit of confronting anyone with whom he has a disagreement. In many ways it is an admirable trait, and it arises, we are forced to believe, out of that same high courage which has always distinguished him. Mr. Baca may not be called a great man and it cannot be denied that he has frequently labored mightily in a bad cause, but nobody can truthfully say that he has ever lacked courage. It is part of the romanticism of the man, combined with his genuine bravery, which has led him in half a dozen episodes of his life, to antici-pate trouble much as he did in the case of Numero Ocho.

It is as well to end this chapter with an in-stance of Mr. Baca's good common sense. It hap-pened that during his reign at the Tivoli he threw a certain young man into the *jusgado*. It was not a rare occurence, but this was a different young man. It was, in brief, the son of the chief of po-lice of Juarez. Mr. Baca, as has been hinted, knows a trifle about Mexican politics. He knows also that there is no sense of crying over past deeds. He knew instantly upon learning of the young man's identity that his further usefulness at the Tivoli was ended.

He drew his last $25 at the eleven o'clock ses-sion of the Tivoli and said a hearty farewell to Messrs. Revilla, Rebia, Lopez and Asteca, reading from left to right. They knew why he was going and made no effort to detain him. He knew that they knew and he made no remonstrance. It was part of life in Old Juarez. He had made many good arrests and he made one good arrest which had turned out not so good. It was part of fate. Adios, Senor Revilla! Adios, Senor Rebia! Adios,

Senor Asteca! Adios, everybody! Good luck to you!

Elfego returned to the peace and contentment of New Mexico.

CHAPTER FIFTEEN

Albert Bacon Fall

No history of Elfego Baca and no history of New Mexico could be written without mention of Albert Bacon Fall.

Politics in New Mexico has always been the principal industry of the State. Its extent in area, its mountains, its ancient ruins, its history and its barren mesas affect the New Mexican almost wholly in a political way. It makes the vote late in getting in. In New Mexico there are seven hundred voting precincts extending over an area larger than the New England states, New York and New Jersey combined.

Politics had always been a worthy game in our state, but it never attained its true stature until Bull Andrews read Horace Greeley's advice to young men and advanced on us from Pennsylvania. The advent of Bull marked the modern phase. To Bull is conceded the honor of so thoroughly corrupting a large percentage of the native and Anglo vote that many of our good citizens are yet afraid to vote without compensation, fearing it to be illegal. The idea is dying rapidly, however, be it said, and New Mexico is becoming more wide awake in industrial lines and a bit less avid of politics every year.

The system up to the arrival of Mr. Andrews had been based on the control of the Dons over their vassals. Upon the breaking up of the huge Spanish land grants had ensued the era of the *patron*. The *patron* was usually an influential citizen of Spanish descent who exerted his efforts to getting control of the water in the ditch. Votes came easy after that. No vote, no water, no rancho. It was into this atmosphere that Albert Fall came from Kentucky as an arden Democrat. The virgin flame of Democracy burned a good many years. How it flickered and died is part of this tale.

It was a gradual change, forsooth, for young Fall was engaged more steadily in the beginning in a struggle for existence. Going through the various stages of prodding homesick Texas steers into the path of right, Fall was in turn cowpuncher, section hand, starving lawyer and prospector. Among other things he went through the glorious year of 1893, beloved of New Mexico history, when lambs sold for 85 cents a head. This quite knocked all thoughts of the remunerativeness of the law or anything else from the head of young Fall. He betook himself into the wilderness in the company of another helpless young man by the name of Edward L. Doheny, who had been struck at almost the same instant by the glory of regular meals.

The hungry young men dug away a large part of Southern New Mexico in search of hidden wealth, and collected specimens enough to fill the

Smithsonian Institute. Specie in exchange was not forthcoming, however, and they wended their way back to Alamogordo with their stomachs groaning loudly enough to be heard above the passing trains. They sought anew the comfort of the mooing herd. They punched cattle during the years 1894-95-96, with Fall at intervals deigning to become a votary of the law and Doheny with the ever present urge of the prospector dashing off into nowhere in quest of what always turned out to be nothing.

As the saying goes, times were hard—and meals far between. Mr. Fall had made up his mind that food at stated intervals around the family board was an ambition to be harbored by every young man of sense. He desired very ardently to return to Kentucky, but there were difficulties. He had not attained the dignity of a railroad pass and his days of cow punching had spoiled him for walking. He was, as the phrase has it, stranded. But something came to his rescue almost immediately: the Spanish-American War.

Mixed with a definite strain of belligerency which has always characterized him, Fall was obsessed by a desire of getting out of the state of New Mexico. There was no time to be lost. He grabbed his choicest pony, hotfooted it into Alamogordo, uttered a few whoops as he dashed down the lone street and paused to make a patriotic speech in front of the saloon. They organized a cavalry troop in fifteen minutes and elected Fall Captain.

Like many another one, Fall never got nearer Cuba than the swamps of Georgia. Two years of war in that setting made him more tolerant of New Mexico shortcomings, and he returned to become a public man.

It was a harsh political school in which Albert Fall and Elfego Baca were reared. The crux of it was the Spanish-American and such men as Fall and H. O. Bursum came to have uncanny sway over the native vote. Fall and Bursum followed such astute politicians as T. B. Catron and the original Stephen B. Elkins, who made a comfortable fortune as lawyer and trader in Santa Fe before returning to become Czar of West Virginia.

The Spanish-American politician is a great "front runner." It takes a persistent winner and a steady supply of jobs to keep his affection. New Mexico was a territory with officers appointed by the current regime in Washington. Except for the two Cleveland administrations there were long years of lean pickings for the Democrats. Such men as H. B. Fergusson, N. C. Collier, N. B. Laughlin, and W. C. Childers kept the Democratic organization alive and in several instances succeeded in electing a Democratic representative to Congress.

But with the Republican National Government steadily in the saddle, it was losing fight. Fall, always keen for reason, sensed the inevitable. He became a Republican in due course and forgot about Kentucky.

The one great source of power in a western state is the Land Office and there was no little thing about the Land Office that Fall was not aware of. The cattlemen with the need of good grazing land and water holes, were at the mercy of the Land Commissioner. Strangely enough, there were never any acceptable lands to be found by a Democratic ranchman. Good grazing leases went where they would bring political returns. The Republican organization became impregnable. Fall was successively member of the State Legislature, Justice of the State Supreme Court, twice Attorney-General of the State, and a member of the Constitutional Convention when New Mexico became a state.

All other honors paled before the latter. Fall *was,* in few words, the Constitutional Convention. He was at the heighth of his power in New Mexico. "Albert Bacon Fall" was a name reserved for the Tea Pot Dome exposures. At the time of the Constitutional Convention he was plain A. B. Fall—dynamic, ruthless, overwhelming. Never tender with the feelings of others, he rode cowboy fashion over opposition outside and within his party. To Bursum had been left the work of organization. It was Bursum who had a seat reserved for himself at the rear of both the House and the Senate during sessions of the Legislature. He never sought election for himself, but his chair was waiting for him. No bill could be brought up, no bill could be passed without the Bursum o. k. Which meant as well the approval of A. B. Fall.

Fall governed the Constitutional Convention with the famous edict: "The people paying the most taxes deserve the most consideration." It meant that the railroad interests, the cattle interests and the coal and copper interests were to rule New Mexico. To make certainty positive the Constitution was so constructed that amendment was literally impossible in almost every case and not possible in any case until after the lapse of twenty five years. Even the Republican administration of Taft could not stomach this and the famous New Mexico blue ballot corrected it, but the intent remained.

This was one side of Fall's character—the conviction that business had rights not necessary to the individual. The other side even more valid, was friendship—the friendship and loyalty of one party man to another. Fall is a forthright man. He is your friend to the hilt; he is your enemy to death. A fullblooded man of explosive downrightness, he made his stand and was not swerved. Help Fall, gain his good will and his last cent was yours. Oppose him and prepare to defend yourself against all form of attack. It was the code of the range, of the old line politician, of the early miner.

It was the code that applied to Elfego Baca and every other loyal Republican. Joined to it all in Fall was ability of a high order. Consider the man—a new United States Senator from a powerless state, New Mexico. Elected in 1912, practically unknown, and rising before 1918 to a place of high prominence in the Senate.

He was a leader in the League of Nations fight and became known as an expert on international law. It is not generally known but he was offered the post of Secretary of State upon the advent of President Harding. Fall refused that honor because his political sense made him realize the furore that would follow the appointment, but he sat as Secretary of the Interior the same A. B. Fall who had governed New Mexico. He was still the A. B. Fall of ''My friends right or wrong; to hell with my enemies.''

Then came the oil leases, the private car of Harry Sinclair on the siding at Three Rivers, the black satchel of Doheny, the money strewn on a table in the back room of a little New Mexico bank, the improvements at the Three Rivers ranch. The nation was shocked, but Fall's friends in New Mexico looked on in astonishment. What was all the shooting for? Why in the name of sense shouldn't Fall give leases to Ed Doheny? Hadn't they been grub mates in the days when they were both as poor as Mexican sheepherders? Doheny had plenty of money—what was a hundred thousand dollars from him to help out an old friend?

So said the intimate New Mexico friends of A. B. Fall in bewilderment at the roar of the press. They remain bewildered to this day. For a while under the pressure there appeared to be a hazy realization that Fall had acted foolishly if not criminally, but with the passing of time that has given way to a feeling akin to resentment. They appear to be angry with Fall for taking so little when he could have got so much more.

If it were not for the black satchel and the mysterious manner of the money transactions even Fall's enemies in New Mexico might be convinced that Fall himself was unconscious of wrong doing in the oil lease matter. It was again: "Anything for a friend; to hell with my enemies."

The point may be labored, but it could be insisted that you cannot understand the full meaning of Fall's action unless you know New Mexico. It is the most political of States. The Spanish-American is a born politician. Politics is a world in itself, with a philosophy of its own. It is the world of political favors, of expediency, of "loyalty". For twenty years Fall was king in that world.

It is perhaps best exemplified by Fall's experiences in Mexico. The ousting of Diaz and the disturbances following had resulted in severe losses for Fall. In an effort to put his mining ventures

Captain Garibaldi, descendant of the Italian hero, who helped Madero in the Mexican Revolution. Garibaldi (figure in the center wearing cartrage belt and revolver); Madero on extreme right.

back on their feet he had supported various Mexican regimes—among them Huerta's. When Villa annihilated the Huerta forces at Ojinaga in January 1914, it really meant the end of the Huerta adventure. Huerta continued to struggle, but his hopes to return to power were all so much wasted endeavor, as a man of Fall's acumen could see. There was nothing more to be gained by being good to Huerta. The thing to do—as most of them were doing—was to desert the Huerta bandwagon precipitately and hasten aboard another.

But Huerta, maligned, despised and an outcast, died in Fall's home in El Paso, the sole refuge for an old, beaten man.

Fall had striven mightily for United States recognition of Huerta. That failing he now fought Carranza and Villa without thought of compromise. The tactics used against Carranza were not nice tactics. They were, in truth, highly unfair and vicious tactics. But Carranza was an enemy. It was poor policy for a United States Senator to harbor the rebel, Huerta, in his home, especially after his political strength was gone. But Huerta was a friend.

"Anything for a friend; to hell with our enemies."

The philosophy of Albert Bacon Fall.

CHAPTER SIXTEEN

"Bull" Andrews Descends on New Mexico

Elfego Baca is given credit in some quarters for electing Fall to the United States Senate on his first attempt. It was before the day of direct election of senators, and the vote in the legislature was a deadlock. With money flowing freely it was to be supposed that some would be used in ways other than legitimate. Elfego is credited with trapping four legislators in such a way as to preclude the possibility of denial that they had accepted a bribe to vote against Fall. The unseating of the culprits next day gave Fall the margin he needed.

And Elfego is one who still retains a friendly feeling for the Secretary of Interior.

"Fall was all right", says Elfego. "It was Andrews. He's the one who corrupted New Mexico. 'Bull' Andrews, you know I told you about him."

Yes, Mr. Baca and dozens of others have related the fiscal wonders of Mr. Andrews.

"Before he came nobody knew how to sell a vote," continues Elfego. "A man running for office, he would go out, riding in a buggy, probably. 'Mr. Armijo', he would say, meeting a man. 'Mr. Armijo, I want you to vote for me'. "Mr. Del-

gado', Mr. Armijo would say, 'Mr. Delgado, I am
very sorry but I have promised to vote for Mr.
Chavez.' 'That is perfectly all right, Mr. Armijo,'
Mr. Delgado would say, 'but next time maybe if
I run, I want you to vote for me'. And Mr. Armijo would nod and say, 'Next time I will surely vote
for you, Mr. Delgado, if you run'."

And the native Spanish-American was noted
for keeping his word. "Bull" Andrews came into
the state soon after relinquishing his position as
first lieutenant to the famous Matt Quay of Pennsylvania. He immediately began to let New Mexico politics into the Quay secrets.

His first venture was at Hillsboro, where he
located on arrival. "Bull" ran for State Senator
and started his campaign by donating $2,500 to the
Republican party fund; he followed that up by a
donation of $1,000 to the Democratic party fund,
and managed to squeeze out an additional $500 for
an independent movement that was threatening.
Mr. Andrews became State Senator.

His next ambition was to be delegate to Congress from the Territory of New Mexico, and it
was then that he really established himself in New
Mexico fame. To begin with he got the nomina-
tion by methods more effective than ethical, and
he followed it up by a campaign so spectacular
that it will probably never be forgotten in the unfortunate state he selected as his final political
jousting ground. The last two weeks of the cam-

paign were featured by the Andrews special train,
one car of which was given over to a dispensary.
The regulation campaign cigars were supplement-
ed by fancy cigarettes, and there were candies and
fruits and flowers and toys for the children and
something for both young and old. It was a triumphal tour of Homo Bountiful.

But that was only a minor part of the entertainment. The *piece de resistance* consisted of
three boxes. Box number one was stuffed full of
—you'll never guess—one dollar bills! Box number two was loaded to the gills with two dollar
bills! Box number three—equally as large, report
has it—was filled to suffocation with five dollar
bills!

It is estimated that Mr. Andrews and his
assistants dispensed an average of five hundred
dollars a day in the month before election. How
true this is will probably never be known at this
late day, but it can be agreed that there must have
been considerable fire to have caused the smoke
that enveloped the tour of the Andrews Election
Special. Mr. Andrews went back to the same Congress where he had spent many happy days chas-
ing back and forth between the room in which Mr.
Quay worked and the dais on which Uncle Joe
Cannon sat.

There is a story quoted in this regard about
the experience of Mr. Cannon, Mr. Quay and Mr.
Andrews with a bill which was intended to make

the cost of upper berths in pullmans half the price
of the lower berth.   The Pullman representatives
were agitated and brought the matter to the attention of Mr. Andrews, with the thought that he
would in turn present it to Mr. Quay.   They pointed out the nature of their contributions to the
Republican fund, and, what was more to the nub of
things, also gave it as their opinion that the pro-
posed law on the face of it was unfair.   What, in
short, could Mr. Andrews do about it?

"For a pint of cider," said Mr. Andrews inelegantly and mayhap facetiously, "I'll see the old
man and do what I can."

He proceeded to the office of Mr. Quay and
presented the matter.

"Let's see the bill," said the gentleman.

He read it through.

"Well, what about it?" he said.

"It's a bad bill and the Pullman people want
you to help them with it.   You know what they've
done to help us."

"It *is* a bad bill," said Mr. Quay, with the
authority that came from perusing many bad bills.
"What do you want me to do about it?"

"Well, it's on the calendar in the House today and they're going to pass it if we don't hold it
up," said Mr. Andrews.

"You go over," said Mr. Quay, "you go over
and tell Cannon I said throw this bill out the window."

"To throw a bill out the window" meant to heave it into the ash heap or at least hold it up for further discussion.

So "Bull" went over to the House to interview Mr. Joe Cannon who sat in state on the rostrum and alternately aimed distributions from his chew at a hidden receptacle and whanged the gavel before him with vigor. Mr. Andrews, not being allowed to approach nearer the sacred precincts than the lower steps leading up to it from the rear, brought the matter of the Pullman bill to Mr. Cannon's attention from that position.

"Matt sent me over to tell you this Pullman bill on the calendar is not right, and to ask you to throw it out the window."

"Uncle Joe", with his eyes glued on the splendid body of men before him, gave no sign. But suddenly "Bull" heard words issuing from the corner of the Cannon face.

"Andrews," said "Uncle Joe," aiming a wad at the spittoon, and rapping the gavel sharply for order, and never looking around to where Andrews was. "Andrews," he declared out of the corner of his mouth while he continued to hold sway over the august assemblage of the House of Representatives of the United States of America, "Andrews," said Mr. Cannon, "Dam your soul; you're lying!"

"Wham!" went the gavel, as the Speaker of

the House called to order an obstreperous gentleman from Georgia or Indiana or elsewhere.

But Mr. Andrews persisted in the face of all doubt and finally convinced "Uncle Joe" that the message was authentic and that the bill was a very bad bill and should be thrown out the window. And out the window it was thrown in due time.

Others may have forgiven Bull Andrews but Elfego Baca is not among them. The lesson begun then has been difficult to unlearn. The use of money is becoming less common every year, but there are still precincts where the five dollar bill is as potent as of yore. Fortunately enough the ruin of the habit lies within itself, and it will take only a few years more for it to encompass its own downfall. The politicians have suddenly learned to their dismay that the "Anglo" voter who accepts a five dollar gratuity is not always an honorable upright gentleman. He will take five dollars from you, and five dollars from me, and go his own sweet way in the matter of voting. The Spanish-American *au contraire* is honest in his graft, say the politicians. If he takes your five dollars you can almost be certain that he is going to vote for you. With the "Anglo" it is an unpleasant and unprofitable gamble. He may or he may not, and be damned to you. It is not likely that the Spanish-American will be affected in the same manner, but if he ever should the era of the five dollar bill will be at an end in New Mexico, and party funds then will have to be expended solely in influencing the few and to providing ''publicity,'' and party ''workers'', and other clever accessories into which the conspicuously honest funds of other enlightened states go.

Which is another way of saying that politics in New Mexico has never been worse than elsewhere, but simply more romantic.

CHAPTER SEVENTEEN

ELFEGO MEDITATES ON MR. MAGEE

There is no room in this history for the innumerable times the gun of Elfego Baca was dragged forth in anticipation of trouble, and no room for the total of rumpuses that were headed off by such promptitude.

Elfego was in El Paso when a telegram came asking him to be a speaker at a meeting of the Cattle Growers' Association to be held in Magdalena. He went and duly presented his few remarks.

Following the sessions of the association was a grand *baile* attended by the better part of Magdalena and honored by the presence of the guests to the convention. Mr. Elfego Baca went not because he was enamoured of the art of Terpsichore or because he had any intention of practising it, but because a proper invitation is something that deserves attention. He remained on the outskirts of the dance in as much seclusion as a man of his reputation can ever hope to attain at a public gathering.

The group in which he was standing was suddenly broken asunder by the appearance of an American cowboy who headed straight for Mr.

Baca and accosted him rudely with the following words:

"You ain't agoin' ta run this dance!"

"Me?" said Elfego mildly. "Me—run the dance? Who said I wanted to run the dance?"

"You might think you are, but you ain't goin' ta run this dance!" said the blustery individual, breasting up to Elfego and sticking his jaw well forward in aggression.

"Who said I wanted to run the dance?" said Mr. Baca. "What the hell's the matter with you?"

"I'll show you what's the matter, you dirty . . . .", said the cowboy, dropping his hand to his hip and preparing to drag forth his miniature cannon.

"Bam!" went the fist of Elfego against the jaw of the boisterous cowboy, depositing him in a heap on the slippery dance floor.

When the excitement had died down, Elfego found himself amid a crowd which blocked the entrance to the dance hall. Among the spectators was one Bill Saunders, with a record of three notches on his gun and a total disdain for the general run of white men. Elfego knew Saunders. He was also curious to know the source of the recent disturbance.

"Who," said Elfego to Bill Saunders, "who was the fellow who just tried to get gay with me?"

Saunders whirled, grabbed for his guns, and

gritted between his teeth; "A damned sight better man than you, you . . . ."

Saunders—as had been his friend before—was a trifle late.

Elfego's gun was pressed tight to Saunders' ribs before the latter had time to more than get his hand on the gun which rested on his hips.

"Yup! Yup! Damn you, and keep them up!"

Elfego goaded Saunders in the ribs and headed him around into the circle of light that came from the dance hall door. With the facility that came from handling wild men in the same mood, Elfego relieved Saunders of his guns while giving him no chance to get active on his own behalf. He added to the gaiety of the occasion by suddenly grasping Saunders by the shoulder, whirling him around and kicking him soundly in the rear with one vicious drive from his boots. It was ignominy piled on to misfortune, and Saunders was not a pretty sight to behold.

If deep murder were in the heart of Saunders, deep rage was as well in the heart of Elfego Baca. He conceived the whole affair as a plot to kill him, and he was in a mood to tempt fate. Going back to his room at the hotel, he accumulated his extra gun, and prepared to return to the scene of the fracas. The hotel proprietor attempted to stop him.

"You go back down there, and that bunch'll get you," he said, coming in from the street fresh with news of the late events. "Saunders is raving, and his gang is posted. Stay here, and maybe you'll have a chance."

"The hell with them," said Elfego. "I'm going back."

Which he did—going straight to the saloon where he knew he would find Saunders and his gang.

As he appeared abruptly in the door of the saloon, he saw Saunders—in the same motion—grab for his gun and try to get around behind the protection of the bar.

"Drop it!" said Elfego tensely. Which was enough to get the action he needed. The gun of Saunders clattered to the floor and he came around in plain sight of Elfego, who carefully kept the saloon crowd between the bar and himself.

"Come on up," commanded Elfego. "This is on me. Everybody drinks. You don't know me, do you? .... I'm a Texas cowboy. .... I'm bad. .... Come on up. Drink!"

He laid one big gun out on top of the bar and kept a kindly eye on his guests, who were now breasted up to the tongue-loosening establishment enjoying his hospitality.

"Another one! commanded the insatiable Elfego, who was quite evidently in no mood for argument. "Set 'em up! Drink! I'm a Texas cowboy. .... I'm bad. .... None of these damn

Mexicans for me. . . . . Texas. . . . . That's me. . . . .
Drink!''

Considering the matter from all angles they
decided it was just as well to partake of the refreshments offered by Mr. Baca. They drank,
and tried not to be conscious of the attentive eye
of Elfego, which seemed smiling on the exterior
and made of hard flint deep down.

They drank once, and they drank again.

''These,'' said Elfego waving an insouciant
hand at the empty glasses on the bar, and addressing the proprietor who stood behind all bedecked
in white apron and ingratiating manner. ''These
have been very good drinks. I wish to thank you
for them, Mr. Allen.''

Mr. Allen beamed his thanks.

''I'm so happy you like them, Mr. Baca.''

''Excellent indeed, Mr. Allen,'' said Elfego.
''I am deeply indebted to you. Your guests are
deeply indebted to you, I am sure. You are without doubt one of the most hospitable men Magdalena has ever had the pleasure of possessing.''

It was beginning to dawn on Mr. Allen that
all was not well.

''Why-uh,'' began Mr. Allen.

''You surely,'' said Mr. Baca, anticipating
him. ''You surely don't expect me . . . . ? A
Texas cowboy. . . . . That's me. . . . . These damn
Mexicans, now . . . . But a Texas cowboy, like me
. . . . You surely don't . . . .''

Mr. Baca left the question hanging lightly in the air, the while he toyed with his guns and fixed Mr. Allen with a smiling eye which had nothing of mirth in it for Mr. Allen.

"Certainly not, Mr. Baca," said Mr. Allen hastily. "Cer-tain-ly not." And gave up all thought of remuneration.

Mr. Baca accordingly departed to carry out the same program in other saloons of Magdalena. It was his fond hope that Bill Saunders would so far forget his modestly as to step forward and start something. Bill Saunders was quite content to keep out of sight.

Saunders was still absent when Elfego left next morning for Socorro. Mr. Baca left with as much ostentation as was possible and asked on every hand the whereabouts of Mr. Saunders. They were, said the friends of Mr. Saunders, un-known—quite, entirely unknown.

Elfego had been in Socorro a week and had almost forgotten the Magdalena incident when rumors reached his ears that Bill Saunders was looking for him. Looking for him with evil intent, so rumor ran. In fact Bill Saunders had raced down the main street of Magdalena the day after Elfego had left and demanded sight of that Mexican this and that, Elfego Baca. By the gods, if he could only get sight of said Elfego Baca what dire things would happen. Bill Saunders was a bad man, and a man who craved nothing other than one look at the Baca who had but lately fled from Magdalena rather than face one Bill Saunders.

Before Elfego could do anything about it, a kindly friend of Mr. Saunders proceeded at top speed to Socorro to intercede on behalf of peace and good will.

"Don't pay any attention to what Saunders says," begged the friend, appealing to Elfego, who was super-heated around the collar and literally champing to be on the trail of the Saunders person. "Bill was drunk when he did that. He didn't know what he was saying."

"He didn't apologize about it, did he?" said Elefgo pointedly. "He didn't waste any breath telling people he was a liar when he said those things."

"No-o," admitted the friend.

"Well," said Elfego, "I'm getting tired of Bill Saunders. It's either him or me. You can go back and tell him this: He can settle it just as soon as he wants to. He can take his gun and I'll take mine, and you can lock us in a room. The man who comes out can live in Socorro County in peace. Either that or you can lock us in a room without any guns. Either way. Only one of us has to get out of Socorro County. It ain't big enough for both of us. You go back and tell Bill that . . . . and more than that; tell him this: Tell Bill that if he don't want to be locked in a room with me, he might as well keep awake nights waiting for me because I'm coming to shoot . . . . I'm damn sick and tired of that hombre . . . ."

The result being that Mr. Saunders decided business prospects were far more promising in California than in New Mexico and soon after left for that Eldorada of the West Coast.

Although it belongs to a much earlier period of Mr. Baca's life we should like to include here an episode which has always interested us. It has to do with his financial state soon after his experiences at Frisco.

Young Baca, at that time and later, was apt to be long on ambition but short on funds. It was a characteristic of the old Southwest that men were seemingly incapable of retaining species of the realm about their persons much longer than it would take to find a place to get rid of it. A man with a thousand dollars about him would be unable to sleep nights until it was spent. This was true in the early days and is true now with many of the old-time stockmen. Money was invented for one purpose only: to stimulate trade. It was meant to be spent, and the young men of the Southwest were loyal to an idea. When they had money they spent it; when they had none they tried to get it.

At the time we speak of, Elfego was broke.

There were two places possible in Socorro that a loan might be raised. One was at the estab-

A picture of great historical importance, showing Madero, Carranza, Orozco and Villa when they were friends. Huerta was present, but not in the picture. (1) Madero; (2) Abran Gonzales, governor of Chihuahua; (3) General Pascual Orozco; (4) Francisco Villa; (5) Francisco Madero, father of Madero; (6) L. Madero, brother of Madero; (7) Garibaldi; (8) Carranza.

lishment of the Price Brothers, private bankers. The other, for Elfego, was from his uncle, Esteban Baca, who operated a general store. Elfego was well aware that his chances of borrowing even nine dollars from Eddie Price were about seven million to one. They were about the same with his uncle, Esteban. But Elfego had a clever idea.

The idea hinged upon the fact that Eddie Price was as deaf as a post.

Elfego proceeded to the store of his uncle with a face on him as sad and long as a builder's lien.

"What's the matter Elfego?" asked his uncle, slightly shocked by such grief. "Why so sad?"

"I'm sad," said Elefgo bravely, "I'm sad because a man just insulted you."

"Insulted me!" shouted the elder Mr. Baca heatedly.

"Yes," admitted Elfego even more sadly.

"What man?" bellowed the irate grocer.

"Eddie Price," said Elfego. "He said he wouldn't take your name on a note for fifteen cents!"

"WHAT!" shouted Esteban, who was one of Price's best accounts.

"Yes," went on Elfego hastily. "I wanted to borrow five hundred dollars and he asked who my security was, and I said you, and he said he wouldn't take your name on a note for fifteen

cents. He said your name wasn't good for nothing.''

The elder Mr. Baca was reaching for his hat
and heading for the door.

''You come with me!'' he yelled, and the parade started for the establishment of Eddie Price.

Mr. Price was in the rear of his place when
the Bacas entered. Mr. Baca irately wrote a check
for five hundred on the blanks of Mr. Price, signed
''Esteban Baca'' with a flourish, and pounded on
the ledge before the solitary wicket in the Price
private bank. Mr. Price, in his deafness, could
discern a slight commotion in his rear and turned
to face the bubbling Mr. Baca. He came forth
beaming, to face the clenched fist of the elder Mr.
Baca waving before his eyes. Mr. Price knew not
what to make of it, but he saw the check—the
perfectly good check—of Esteban Baca.

''My name no good, eh!'' shouted Mr. Baca.
''Well, you cash that check there as fast as you
can or take the consequences!''

''Why, Mr. Baca . . . . . '', protested
Price, understanding the gestures but not the
words, and counting out the coin necessary to ap-
pease the old man.

He pushed it across the counter, still bewildered and a great deal frightened. The elder Mr.
Baca took the bills grandly and handed them to
the younger Mr. Baca without taking his eyes
from the face of Mr. Price.

The younger Mr. Baca took the money, assisted the general air of tenseness by also casting sundry dirty looks in the direction of the now thoroughly abashed Mr. Price, and got his uncle out of the bank as if to avert a disastrous clash. He wanted the elder Mr. Baca away before Eddie Price could get around to the exchange of billet douxs which passed as conversation in the Price place. Mr. Esteban Baca departed waving a belligerent fist and throwing fresh Spanish insults over his shoulder at every step.

They left a mightily bewildered and saddened Mr. Price in their wake.

We should like also to relate an incident which concerns Carl C. Magee, the former Albuquerque editor whose journalistic battles kept New Mexico astir for many a year.

Elfego was never able to understand how Magee kept alive through those experiences. The editor was whacking heads right and left and was anything but careful of whom he attacked. He assaulted men and combinations of men with such vehemence as to arouse the most violent retaliation. As a consequence he ran into libel charges and later charges of contempt of court.

The first time Mr. Magee was haled off to court in Las Vegas, where his official friends were few and far between, Elfego went down to the train to see him off. He shook him by the hand sadly. He knew that Mr. Magee, an Albuquerque editor, was to be tried in a Las Vegas court for alleged libel against a judge living in Santa Fe. He knew what that meant not only as a general thing but from personal knowledge of the gentlemen who governed the Kingdom of San Miguel, in which Las Vegas is situated.

"Good-bye, Mr. Magee," said Elfego, and his voice was anything but cheerful.

"Good-bye, Elfego; I'll see you when I get back."

"No, you won't," said Elfego.

"Why? . . . . Won't you be here?" asked Mr. Magee.

"Yes, I will, but you won't."

And Elfego was freshly dumfounded every time he saw Mr. Magee alive during those hectic times.

In those days Mr. Baca had offices in the Sunshine building in Albuquerque, which faced the corner of Second and Central. From his windows Elfego had an unobstructed view of the intersection of the two streets and at least half a block down South Second. He was sitting by the window one Spring day conversing with a client when he saw Mr. Magee coming up Second street toward Central.

"Just look at him," said Elfego, disgustedly. "Walkin' along there with his head down and just coaxin' somebody to take a pot shot at him . . . ."

He sat and looked at the figure of Mr. Magee as it made its way slowly up the street.

"I could sit right here in this chair with a rifle," he meditated aloud, "and ping! ping! I could shoot him in the temple without anybody ever knowin' what had happened."

He drew an imaginary bead on the distant figure and appeared to consider the matter seriously.

"Just two shots," said Mr. Baca gravely, and turned about in his chair and waved his hand lightly, as if to show how simple it would be. "And to hell with the bloodhounds!"

CHAPTER EIGHTEEN

A Short Sermon on Various Things

In all that has gone before and in that which is about to follow, we have perhaps made more of the spectacular side of Elfego Baca's life than is warranted. There is danger that the fact of his record of a lawyer and a public man will be overlooked, and that would be unjust to him.

Mr. Baca read law in the office of Judge Hamilton at Socorro and was admitted to the bar in December 1894. In February 1895, the law firm of Freeman and Baca was organized. Judge Freeman, being but recently Associate Judge of the Supreme Court of New Mexico, the firm had a standing of high rank from the start. Judge Freeman was a jurist of rare distinction in any company, and his decision in the case of Hargrave vs Smith is said by lawyers to be without equal in the annals of jurisdiction in this country. It is listed in the index of the New Mexico decisions of the supreme court under HUMOR, and we can testify as a layman that it is one of the most subtly and devastatingly humorous pieces of writing ever fashioned. That it should come from a judge on the bench is even more marvelous. It shows a mind of the highest type and an imagination so fertile as to make one wish that the law had never held him.

It has always seemed to us that nothing so stamped the mark of approval on Elfego Baca as a young attorney as the fact that Judge Freeman considered him worthy to be a partner. Mr. Baca has had a long and varied career in the New Mexico courts, and was admitted to practice before the United States Supreme Court in 1919. His experience in the case of General Salazar led to his appearance before the congressional committee which was investigating the claims of Huerta to recognition. In all fairness it would not do to speak of Mr. Baca as a great lawyer. He has always been hampered in the courts by his lack of fluency in English, but his record as a criminal lawyer has been of the highest, and he is credited with securing the acquittal of nineteen individuals charged with murder.

As has been set out in the foreword, there are many incidents in the life of Mr. Baca which we have not felt of sufficient interest to warrant preservation in this volume. Among them is the capture of Jose Chavez y Chavez, the notorious bandit leader of San Miguel County, who was taken by Mr. Baca in the southwest part of Socorro County. There is also the incident of the German who stole a valuable automobile at Las Cruces and went through Socorro with it. Elfego followed in another and slower car and was on the verge of giving up the chase when the car ahead suddenly stopped, its gasoline tank being punctured and drained by Mr. Baca's chance shots.

It would be possible to devote a chapter to the mining activities of Mr. Baca. He entered the business around Magdalena and Mogollon, and came to have a reputation in estimating the worth of properties. He later represented several large companies at Guanajuato and Parral, Mexico, and there gained his first personal knowledge of the men who were fated to lead Mexico through its successive revolutions. It was at Parral that he had his closest escape from death when he was descending an abandoned mine on a ladder that broke and hurled him forty feet to the bottom of the shaft. He had gone by himself because he wanted to see the property before it might be tampered with by owners anxious to sell it to American capitalists. He lay in the pit the best part of a day before he regained consciousness and could manage to make his way up that part of the ladder which still remained. It was a harrowing experience that lingers in his mind to this day in a way that none of his shooting escapades has.

In his various political perigrinations, Mr. Baca has been stabbed by a dagger, shot at innumerable times and stabbed by an ice pick with very serious results. It is not so far in the past when he was run over by a fire wagon on Central avenue in Albuquerque. It was an injury that should by all rights have finished him, but it failed of its purpose. It bunged him up badly, but it had no more effect in stopping him than did a later automobile accident on the road to Santa Fe.

There would seem to be no better place than this to discuss the Spanish of New Mexico as a race. The Mexican has been maligned in picture and tale, and the discredit gained in that wise has been wished on the Spanish-American as well. In neither case do we feel that it is justified, and we are especially resentful of any attempt to make the Spanish-American out as anything but the gentle, kind-hearted, fair minded individual that he is. We are not one to feel that because a man keeps a dog he is incapable of robbing a bank, but it is hard to ascribe the moving picture idea of an underhanded, traitorous, backshooting race to a people that would no sooner think of having a home without a pot of geraniums in every window than it would of attacking the *padre* of their parish. There are exceptions to all rules, and there are many bad Spanish-Americans just as there are bad members of all races, but the generality is as we have given it—a kindly folk of gentle tradition and a life which was in most ways far more livable before it had the benefit of Yankee civilization.

It was with genuine regret that New Mexico mourned the death of Felix Garcia, the merchant of Lumberton. It was Mr. Garcia who had the

habit of receipting the unpaid bills of poor ranchers and sheepherders with the notation: ''Paid in
Full—By God.'' It was anything but a blasphe-
mous utterance. It correctly described the feeling
of Mr. Garcia that God protects us all, that he
looks over all of us, gives us all we have and finally takes it all away. It was Mr. Garcia's way of
saying that God had looked after the bill even
though there was no chance of its ever being paid
in earthly currency. It was the kind hearted way
a fortunate man had of attesting his love for his
less fortunate fellowman.

It is extremely difficult to get at the truth of
various assertions in regard to the Spanish-American and it would certainly not do to reassert the
belief that the Spanish were perfect and content
prior to the advent of the American. It would
perhaps be too much to be compelled to believe
that in those old time days every Spaniard's word
was as good as his bond and that thievery, dis-
honesty and cruelty were unknown. There were
undoubtedly Spaniards of that day of poor reputation just as there still are. It is perhaps true,
however, that the life of the great ranches and
land grants constituted an era which for gentility
and happiness has never had a superior on the
western hemisphere. It disappeared with the
breaking up of the land grants and the coming of
the more shrewd ''Anglo'', and there is danger
that we may read into that halcyon period attri-

butes that it did not possess, but all evidence points to the contrary, and the Spanish-American has a right to grieve over the passing of his dominance.

Our only excuse for this near approach to a sermon is that Elfego Baca from his earliest days has been the idol and the protector of the less fortunate members of his race. He fought for them at Middle Frisco, and on many another occasion, and he seems entitled to the position of respect which he holds among the common people of New Mexico. When he was clerk of Socorro county his fees came from the recording of deeds and mortgages and bills of sale. He announced that during the months of December and January no fees would be charged at his office. It meant that the poor farmer of the county would be spared the spending of a possible $5.00 for a filing fee. It seems a trifling thing, but for one who knows the struggle of the poor Spanish-American with his tiny *rancho,* it was a thing showing generosity of a worthwhile sort. Few public officials are addicted to the little acts which mean so much to the common, hard-working man. They prefer to seek a larger, more heaven-rending sort of gesture.

The reader must excuse us if we seem to grow maudlin over the lowly Spanish-American. He has been a muchly maligned man. He has been called lazy and shiftless and dishonest. It is true that he does not profess nor does he practice the

aggressiveness of the Anglo. His is a different
nature, though not necessarily an inferior one.
What the future of the Spanish-American of New
Mexico will be we do not attempt to say. We know
only that he possesses charming, gentle, hospitable
traits which it should be a crime to see pass from
our daily lives.

The chief significance of Elfego Baca is that
he has been able to meet and hold his own with
the Anglo at his own game. It has marked him
as an outstanding New Mexican, regardless of
how his individual acts may be considered.

CHAPTER NINETEEN

ELFEGO ENJOYS A PROFITABLE JAIL SENTENCE

Like all good New Mexicans, Elfego Baca has finally settled in Albuquerque to spend his remaining years. In past years Elfego has pursued his exciting course almost equally between Socorro and El Paso and Albuquerque, but Albuquerque is to have the distinction of his presence in the future. He is now located in the little building at the corner of Sixth and Gold which housed his journalistic ambitions fifteen years ago and is housing them again.

Albuquerque has seen everything that the Southwest has held from the coming of the first *Conquistadores* to the arrival of the last bespectacled Easterner in a ponderous sombrero that almost overwhelms him and high-heeled boots that almost ruin his tender feet. It is now a well-paved, modern, civilized city of 35,000. It was in days gone past something unique in America.

Albuquerque in the early days had ways of its own, and most interesting ways. It had justice of a calibre not dispensed elsewhere, and it was natural that Elfego Baca in his pilgrimages to the Big City, and in the periods when he departed Socorro to live in Albuquerque, should experience things that seemed anything but proper to him.

One of the rare distinctions held by New Mexico's metropolis in that past day was a night court which convened about one o'clock in the morning or at such time as the idea struck the judge. It was noticeably always convened along about the end of an evening that had been disastrous to the judge's three card monte fortunes.

When that happened, the minions of the law were despatched in the direction of the nearest bar with instructions to corral any likely candidate for the hoose-gow who retained enough coin of the realm to make his presence before the court worthy of notice. So ordered, so done.

In would come the slightly bemuddled gentleman in charge of a burly *gendarme*. The charge would invariably be drunkenness and disorderly conduct, which might include anything from murder to slapping a bartender, or weeping unduly at a sentimental ditty wrung from a jangling mechanical piano. Once at headquarters, the prisoner was carefully searched for deadly weapons, and incidentally his stock of United States species was spread before the gaze of the court officials and carefully counted. He would have, let us say, the total sum of $38.42. Very good; he would be haled before the judge.

"What's the charge?" demands the judge.

"Drunkenness and disordely conduct, yer honor," says the officer.

"But . . . . .," begins the prisoner.

"What's your plea?" demands the judge. "Guilty or not guilty?"

"Why . . . .," begins the poor unfortunate. "Why, uh . . . . "

"Guilty or not guilty," says the judge impatiently.

"Well, not guilty," says the man half defiantly. "I wasn't doin' nothin'."

"He was kickin' up a rumpus in the White Elephant," volunteers the guardian of the law.

"Twenty-five dollars and cost or thirty days in jail!" says the judge, putting an end to conversation.

And, most surprising of all things, twenty-five dollars and costs figured up exactly to $37.42, the prisoner learned to his gratification. Just think of the luck of having within a dollar of enough to pay the fine and keep out of jail! By golly, lucky—that's all. And enough left for a good breakfast.

It was into this midnight court that Elfego was eventually dragged.

In an attempt to rescue Jesus Romero from officers who were taking him to the aforementioned court, Elfego had so forgotten himself as to wallop a policeman over the head with a silver watch of such proportions as to constitute a bludgeon. It was a silver watch of the old potato variety and operated behind the vigor of Mr. Baca it had a distinct propensity of destruction. It took one of Albuquerque's favorite policemen full on the top of the dome and rendered him completely *non compos mentis* for the remainder of the evening. It was then that an avalanche of Albuquerque citizenry reinforced the police force and bore Elfego away on a tide of persuasion. He was rushed into the midnight court in place of "Soos" Romero, who had been forgotten in the rumpus.

"Drunken and disorderly," said the complaint.

"You're crazy," said Elfego.

"Silence!" bellowed the judge, striving to delay matters until the night sergeant could check up on the wealth taken from the pockets of Elfego.

"I know exactly how much I got," said Elfego in a loud aside to the sergeant. "$18.19. If you count a nickel less you'll get yours later and good and plenty."

"Shut up!" said the judge with what he took for judicial dignity.

"Well, wait and see," said Elfego amiably.

"Guilty or not guilty?" asked the court.

"Not guilty!" said Elfego, "and you all know it damn well!"

"Thirty days or ten dollars and costs!" said the judge.

"I suppose ten dollars and costs is $17.19, eh?" said Elfego. "You ain't goin' to pull that stuff on me. I'll take the thirty days."

Which was what he did take—so far as the

Elfego Baca in 1927 at the age of 62 and still very much alive.

judge ever knew. What he took in reality was a pleasant vacation at the expense of the county. This was by reason of the fact that Elfego at the very time of his incarceration in the county jail happened to be jailer of that institution!

Old Albuquerque, where sat the county jail, and New Albuquerque, where sat the celebrated night court, often had little in common, and a jailer was not a person of such distinction as to be known far and wide. The job had been given Elfego as a stop-gap, and nobody in the newer section of Albuquerque was aware that he had it.

He was accompanied to the county jail by a constable of the night court.

At the jail the constable turned Mr. Baca and the committment over to a guard, and hurried back to the game of stud poker he had been dragged from by the plaints of duty. Elfego, dutifully, accepted his own committment from the guard and entered the name of one E. Baca on the prison record. As jailer, Senor Baca received seventy-five cents a day for the feeding of each prisoner. As prisoner Senor Baca received that seventy-five cents for his food. In short, the thirty day sentence that Judge Heacock was so righteously stern in imposing to one E. Baca netted the latter gentleman exactly $22.50 in excess profits. Which surely constitutes one of the most profitable and pleasant prison excursions ever undertaken by mortal man during the late lamented Nineteenth Century.

CHAPTER TWENTY

CONCLUSION. MR. BACA KEEPS VERY MUCH ALIVE

But all this was long ago, and the present is upon us. It is a present that knows nothing of night courts or of the old Albuquerque, and only fleetingly of the figures that made the old days momentous. Only a few of the old timers still retain the reputation or power that once rested with them. Elfego Baca is one of the survivors.

Elfego is in the early sixties and is not the active Elfego of old. Neither is he the ancient Elfego that a man in his sixties has a right to be. It is still not the fashion for young bloods of the southwest to cast any but the kindliest of glances in the direction of Mr. Baca. He is many leagues from being a decrepit old gentleman. He retains in sufficient part the vitality that will allow him— even at this late day—to slap a fresh policeman or kiss a buxom lady.

Politically, Elfego is the Elfego of old. In the campaign of 1924, Mr. Baca desired ardently to accept a position on the Republican ticket in Bernalillo County. Mr. Baca brought these tidings to the convention both in person and with the aid of friends. At the Albuquerque convention of that grand old party, Mr. Elfego Baca was told— in no uncertain terms—to seek a far distant seat and remain in it. He would—said the big bow-wows of the Republican party in Bernalillo county —most certainly *not* be on the Republican slate in the county of Bernalillo. Which was thought— very properly—to be the end of Mr. Baca politically.

Mr. Baca took the back seat, right enough, but he took it only to consider and ponder. From the depths of his deep cogitation came a decision that defeated the Republican candidate for district judge and frightened the fortunately successful Democratic candidate within at least half a foot of his political life.

Mr. Baca was consumed with the notion that there were people yet remaining in New Mexico who had faith in him and friendship for him. Starting two weeks before election without the semblance of an organization and with no funds to create one, Mr. Baca campaigned on his own behalf for the office of district judge for the counties of Bernalillo and Sandoval. Mr. Baca got out a few handbills and made a few energetic speeches. When busy members of the Republican and Democratic organizations had time to consider it, Elfego became the comic relief of the campaign.

Elfego running for district judge! All together now, gentlemen, three loud guffaws! Guf-faws willingly given—without the knowledge or care of Senor Elfego Baca, who was dashing around the county in a second-hand Ford trying to get in as many words as possible to anybody who would listen to him.

In two weeks—unaided except by willing and unexperienced friends—Elfego excited attention to the extent of corralling 3113 votes. Which may not seem a great gathering of the suffrage of the citizens of the counties of Bernalillo and Sandoval, but which was amply sufficient to capsize any chance the regular Republican nominee had, and which came close to doing the same thing for the winning Democrat. It is the opinion of competent political observers that a month's campaign might have put Mr. Baca across.

In the midst of some remarkable orations delivered during the heat of the campaign, Mr. Baca pointed with just pride to his past record. Mr. Baca—so relates the record—was successively county clerk of Socorro County, Mayor of the city of Socorro, District Attorney for the counties of Socorro and Sierra, and Sheriff of the county of Socorro, and School Superintendent of the county of Socorro. It also relates that Mr. Baca was admitted to practice before the Supreme Court of the United States in 1912.

The record also recounted—succinctly, be it noted—that while Sheriff, Mr. Baca erected a garage, without cost to the county, which would in the open market bring the price of $8,000. This required genius on the part of Sheriff Baca—the record indicates—in that he was required to apprehend such cattle thieves, safe crackers and second story gentlemen who were at the same time gifted as brick-layer, stone mason or mechanic. It was a rather neat task of selection, the record gave one to understand, and the garage is still standing today as a record of Sheriff Baca's astuteness.

From the election arose the formation of Club Elfego Baca, which now is reputed to have a membership of 800 and positively had a weekly paper, "La Tuerca,"—The Nut—so called from the emblem of the club, the Bolt and Nut.

It was as late as the present year, 1928, that Mr. Baca assisted in a matter which is of great importance to New Mexico. The Middle Rio Grande Conservancy district was formed to provide flood control, irrigation and reclamation for the country centering around Albuquerque. Part of the lands affected lie within the Indian pueblos, and Mr. Baca happened to be in Washington at a time when a bitter fight was being made to pass a bill which would allow the government to advance the money for the reclamation of the Indian lands. The bill had passed both the House and the Senate, but had been recalled, and things were in a pretty snarl.

Strenuous efforts for the bill were being made by Senators Bratton and Cutting and Representative Morrow of New Mexico, and equally as strenuous opposition was being offered by the liberal group headed by Senator LaFollette and Senator

Frazier, backed by the Indian Defense Association, which wanted the best contract possible for the protection of the Indians.

The passage of the bill was imperative if the Middle Rio Grande valley was to be saved. Mr. Baca had no special intention of being in Washington at a time when the bill was pending, and gave little thought to the situation until it reached an impasse. He was in the office of Senator Cutting, and the air was purple with despair.

"What's the matter here," said Elfego. "The Senator dead?"

"No .... It's this conservancy bill."

"What's the matter?"

"Well, it comes up for a final vote tomorrow morning, and we're licked."

"Um-m."

And the matter rested there for a full minute, hanging portentously in the air.

"Now, listen," said Mr. Baca finally. "The leader over in the Senate is Senator Curtis, isn't it? ..... Well, now, if I went to see Senator Curtis, would that ......"

There was consternation at the very thought.

"You can't see Senator Curtis!"

"The hell I can't," said Mr. Baca, inelegantly.

They discussed the matter. Engaged in the discussion were Mr. Baca, Edgar Puryear, secretary to Senator Cutting, and Miss Florence Droney, who had been secretary to the late Senator

Andrieus A. Jones for ten years, and who knew
Senate procedure and inside politics as well as
anybody in Washington.

"Mr. Baca," said Miss Droney. "Nobody
could go over and see Senator Curtis about this
bill . . . . He'd order you out of his office. If
you went with a delegation, it might be different;
but no individual could approach him like that on
a pending bill."

"Just get Senator Curtis on the telephone,
and tell him Elfego Baca wants to see him for a
minute tomorrow morning before the Senate con-
venes."

"I'd rather not," said Miss Droney.

"Go ahead, now," said Elfego, and Miss
Droney sat down to the telephone and was con-
nected with Senator Curtis' office and eventually
with him. She gave the message.

"You tell Elfego to be in my office promptly
tomorrow morning at 10:15," came back the voice
of Senator Curtis.

And Elfego was there.

"Good morning, Senator."

"Good morning, Elfego; when were you in
Topeka last?"

"Not since the last time I saw you there—
three years ago. But that isn't what I came to
see you about. I'm interested in that conservancy
bill. That's a good bill, Senator."

"Well, now, Elfego, I don't know . . . . ."

"Senator, I know that Rio Grande like an only child. If this bill doesn't go through, we're all going to be drowned. I knew that valley when every acre was under cultivation. Not a fourth of it can be used now. The river is creeping up on all of it."

"But what can I do, Elfego? Here are half a dozen telegrams, and I've had dozens of letters against it."

The matter at that point became slightly warm, and anyone knowing the downrightness of Mr. Baca's conversation would have been justified in thinking that possibly he might come sliding out the door of the Senator's inner sanctum in some slight confusion. But people are not in the habit of assisting the departure of Mr. Baca, and more than that Elfego and Senator Curtis have been friends since they were boys together in Topeka, and are well acquainted with the queer quirks of one another.

The outcome was that Senator Curtis finally said:

"Well, here's what you can do: You go back and see Senator Cutting and have him see the other New Mexican representatives. If they'll agree to this amendment, we can get this thing settled. Not only that, but I'll talk with the President personally and urge him to sign the bill when it's passed."

And Mr. Baca came back to Senator Cutting's

office, wearing on his lapel a big badge which he had picked off the desk of Senator Curtis. It was inscribed: "Curtis for President".

Whether or not Mr. Baca's intervention was a factor in the passage of the conservancy bill, we shall leave to history to determine. At least he was able to beard Senator Curtis in his office, which is something no one else had the courage to do. It is also a matter of record that Senator Charles Curtis of Kansas is the leader of the Republican party in the United States Senate. It is also a matter of record that the bill passed bearing the Curtis amendment.

In other words, Mr. Elfego Baca is still active. It is not so long since the automobile he was driving from Santa Fe to Albuquerque turned over three times in the soft dirt along the road without injury to the wild driver. It is not so far back that Mr. Baca gave very practical illustration of an opinion he possessed in regard to a prize fight which was brought to a riotous close by an especially putrid decision by the referee. While the brave gentlemen of the audience relieved their wrath in wild howls, Mr. Baca climbed nimbly through the ropes and very definitely punched the referee on the nose.

It has always been thus with Mr. Baca. The direct, simple way has always seemed best. There is so much time wasted in this world, Mr. Baca evidently believes, with the little futilities that get you nowhere. If you think that a certain gentleman has done something that warrants a sock on the jaw, the proper and only decent thing to do if you have regard for your own conscience is to walk up and sock the gentleman on the jaw.

This is the philosophy behind Mr. Baca's actions, be he sheriff or be he editor. "La Tuerca" was dictated almost entirely by Senor Baca, who alternated between Spanish and English so that all his friends might indulge themselves in the wisdom that struggled forth from the columns of the good sheet. It may not have been the greatest achievement known to American Journalism, but it was at least a faithful reproduction of the personality behind it. There are those who wish that Mr. Baca's style were a bit less turgid, but there are none to deny that when Mr. Baca speaks it is Mr. Baca speaking and no other.

During the course of his editorialship Mr. Baca announced the terms on which the populace might get within hailing distance of the gems that fell from the columns of "La Tuerca". Said the editor: "La Tuerca" is two dollars a year to good citizens; five dollars a year to bootleggers; and five dollars a month to Prohibition agents".

Editor Baca also made further editorial comment on his stand on prohibition. "I am in favor," said Mr. Baca, "of light wines and beers and 110 proof whisky."

Which brings us to the close of this valuable

history of Mr. Elfego Baca. There he stands. There he has stood for sixty years. The Spanish-American of New Mexico with all his faults and all his virtues. A trifle over anxious at times in his zeal for Law and Order, but for Law and Order nevertheless.

It is because of this that his present political fortunes are bound up in the Law and Order ticket. Some of his friends and a few of his lesser friends are of the opinion that Mr. Baca's party should be incorporated.

Such an incorporated title, perhaps, as "Law and Order, Ltd."

The *Mexican* *American*

An Arno Press Collection

Castañeda, Alfredo, et al, eds. **Mexican Americans and Educational Change.** 1974
Church Views of the Mexican American. 1974
Clinchy, Everett Ross, Jr. **Equality of Opportunity for Latin-Americans in Texas.** 1974
Crichton, Kyle S. **Law and Order Ltd.** 1928
Education and the Mexican American. 1974
Fincher, E. B. **Spanish-Americans as a Political Factor in New Mexico, 1912-1950.** 1974
Greenwood, Robert. **The California Outlaw:** Tiburcio Vasquez. 1960
Juan N. Cortina: Two Interpretations. 1974
Kibbe, Pauline R. **Latin Americans in Texas.** 1946
The Mexican American and the Law. 1974
Mexican American Bibliographies. 1974
Mexican Labor in the United States. 1974
The New Mexican Hispano. 1974
Otero, Miguel Antonio. **Otero:** An Autobiographical Trilogy. 1935/39/40
The Penitentes of New Mexico. 1974
Perales, Alonso S. **Are We Good Neighbors?** 1948
Perspectives on Mexican-American Life. 1974
Simmons, Ozzie G. **Anglo-Americans and Mexican Americans in South Texas.** 1974
Spanish and Mexican Land Grants. 1974
Tuck, Ruth D. **Not With the Fist.** 1946
Zeleny, Carolyn. **Relations Between the Spanish-Americans and Anglo-Americans in New Mexico.** 1974